BOOK
3

WORDLY WISE
3000®

Direct Academic Vocabulary Instruction

Fourth Edition

Kenneth Hodkinson • Sandra Adams • Erika Hodkinson

EDUCATORS PUBLISHING SERVICE
Cambridge and Toronto

Editorial team: Carolyn Daniels, Marie Sweetman, Erika Wentworth
Cover Design: Deborah Rodman, Karen Swyers
Interior Design: Deborah Rodman

Illustrations: Mike Dammer

Printed in Benton Harbor, MI, in May 2022
ISBN 978-0-8388-7702-9

8 PPG 22

Contents

Welcome to *Wordly Wise 3000*®

You've been learning words since you were a tiny baby. At first, you learned them only by hearing other people talk. Now that you're a reader, you have another way to learn words.

When you read, it's important to know what *every* word means. You can try skipping a word you don't know. But this might cause a problem. Read this sentence:

> *Anyone without a* megtab *will not get into the show.*

If you have no idea of what a *megtab* is, you might not get in. All of a sudden, knowing what that one word means is important!

The more words you know, the better. You will understand more of what you read. *Wordly Wise 3000* can't teach you *all* the words you'll need, but it will help you learn lots of them. It can also help you learn how to learn even more words.

How Do You Figure Out What a Word Means?

What should you do when you come to a word and you think you don't know what it means? Following some easy steps can help you.

Say It

First, sound it out. Then say it to yourself. It might sound like a word you know. Sometimes you know a word in your head without knowing what it looks like in print. So if you match up what you know and what you read—you have the word!

Use Context

If this doesn't work, take the next step: look at the context—the other words and sentences around it. Read this sentence:

> *When it rained, the dog looked for* shelter *under the porch.*

If the word *shelter* doesn't look familiar, look at the words around it. *Rain* and *under the porch* might give you a clue. You might even do a Think-Aloud:

> *I know that if you don't want to get wet outside when it rains, you need to get under something. In this sentence, the dog went under the porch to stay dry. So shelter must mean "something that protects you." Yes, that makes sense in this sentence.*

Use Word Parts

If the context doesn't help, look at the parts of the word. Does it have any parts you know? These can help you figure out what it means. Read this sentence:

> *The* miners *put on their hard hats before going to work.*

If you don't know the meaning of *miner*, try looking at parts of the word. You might know that a *mine* is a place underground where people get coal and other valuable things. A lot of times, *-er* at the end of a word means "a person who does something." For example, a *teacher* teaches in a school. So a *miner* might be someone who works in a mine. You would put on a hard hat if you were going into a mine. That meaning of *miner* makes sense.

Look It Up

If saying the word or using context and word parts don't work, you can look it up. You can find the word in a dictionary—either a book or online—or a glossary.

Nobody knows the meaning of every word, but good readers know how to figure out words they don't know.

Study the words. Then do the exercises that follow.

cylinder

n. An object in the shape of a tube or pipe. It may be solid or hollow.

In the center of the table was a tall glass vase in the shape of a **cylinder,** which was filled with yellow tulips.

examine

v. To look at closely.

When Cora and Chun **examined** the desk, they discovered that the letter they were looking for was gone.

 Examine your shoes and describe them to your partner.

fatal

adj. Causing death.

Eating this pretty white mushroom can be **fatal.**

feature

n. 1. An important or special part of something.

An unusual **feature** of this room is a secret stairway hidden behind this wall.

2. Any part of the face.

One pleasing **feature** of Claude's is his warm smile.

 Describe the feature of your shoes you like best to your partner.

grasp

v. 1. To take hold of something tightly with the hands.

Tina **grasped** the bars on the gym set and pulled herself up.

2. To understand something.

After we **grasped** the directions, it was easy to do the puzzle.

 Tell your partner something you have learned that was easy for you to grasp.

jet

n. 1. A stream of liquid or gas that is forced at high speed through a small opening.

The firefighters directed **jets** of water from the pump truck to the burning house.

2. An airplane that is powered by a jet engine.

The pilot told us what kind of **jet** would be carrying us to the West Coast.

marine

adj. Having to do with the ocean or with ships and boats.

The largest **marine** creature is the blue whale.

 Tell your partner about your favorite marine animal.

scar

n. A mark on the skin that is left after a cut or other wound has healed.

The **scar** on Helen's knee is from the cut she got when she fell off her bicycle.

tentacle

n. A long, thin part that grows out from the head of some sea animals. They use it to hold things or to move from place to place.

The cuttlefish wiggled its **tentacles** to bring the small fish closer.

vessel

n. 1. A ship or large boat.

All the passengers aboard the **vessel** hoped to see a whale or dolphin during the trip.

2. Anything hollow that can be used to hold liquids.

A clay **vessel** filled with lemonade rested on the picnic table in the backyard.

 Discuss with your partner what you could pour from a vessel.

1A Words and Their Meanings

Look at the group of words next to the number. Then circle the letter next to the word that has the same meaning.

1 a stream of liquid under pressure
   (a) tentacle   (b) feature   (c) jet   (d) scar

2 a tube-shaped object
   (a) cylinder   (b) vessel   (c) scar   (d) tentacle

3 a mark left after a wound heals
   (a) feature   (b) scar   (c) tentacle   (d) grasp

4 a special part that stands out

(a) tentacle   (b) vessel   (c) feature   (d) marine

5 a large boat or ship

(a) fatal   (b) marine   (c) tentacle   (d) vessel

Look at the word next to the number. Then circle the letter next to the group of words that has the same meaning.

6 examine

(a) look at carefully   (b) return to

(c) stay away from   (d) put away

7 marine

(a) having to do with sports   (b) having to do with being sick

(c) having to do with horses   (d) having to do with the ocean

8 tentacle

(a) a baby octopus   (b) a hairy spider

(c) a long, thin part growing from some sea animals   (d) a figure with eight sides

9 grasp

(a) let go of   (b) understand

(c) move in circles   (d) cry out

10 fatal

(a) helpless   (b) hard to understand

(c) causing death   (d) being careful

cylinder
examine
fatal
feature
grasp
jet
marine
scar
tentacle
vessel

1B

Just the Right Word

Replace each phrase in bold with a single word (or form of the word) from the word list.

1. *SCAr/* He has a **mark on the skin** left by a fall when he was a child.

2. *CYLiNDEr* The machinist looked at each **object in the shape of a pipe.**

3. Kelly always reads the **having to do with the ocean** report before she sets sail.

4. *GrASP* New to crutches, Lin **took hold tightly of** each one firmly.

5. *FAtAL* His mistake, not **causing death** but serious, made him upset.

1C

Applying Meanings

Circle the letter next to the correct answer.

1. Which of the following can be **fatal?**
   - (a) a smile
   - (b) a car accident
   - (c) a number
   - (d) an award

2. Where would you not expect to find **marine** animals?
   - (a) in an ocean
   - (b) in a sea
   - (c) in a forest
   - (d) in an aquarium

3. Which would be the best way to **examine** a planet?
   - (a) build an arch
   - (b) climb a tower
   - (c) turn on a channel
   - (d) look through a telescope

4 Which of the following might leave a **scar?**

(a) a ghost   (b) a lesson

(c) a fall   (d) a song

5 Which of the following can a person **grasp?**

(a) ideas   (b) wind

(c) smells   (d) smoke

1D Word Study: Nouns and Verbs

A noun names a person, place, or thing. Underline the nouns in the sentences.

1 Squid have eight arms and two tentacles.

2 They can shoot out jets of ink if they are in danger.

A verb tells what action is happening or what someone or something is doing. Underline the verbs in the sentences.

3 We launched our new canoe today.

4 We steered the canoe with paddles.

| cylinder |
| examine |
| fatal |
| feature |
| grasp |
| jet |
| marine |
| scar |
| tentacle |
| vessel |

Monsters of the Deep

The Pacific Ocean is huge. But we see only its surface. Underneath, over half a mile down, is another world. This world is very dark. It is the watery home of the giant squid. These unusual creatures spend their whole lives there. Let us explore deep in the Pacific Ocean. We will go near the northeast coast of New Zealand. There we will learn something of these strange animals.

• • • • • • • • • • • • •

Many scientists come to this area. They know it is a good spot to find giant squid. They also find sperm whales there. Sperm whales feed on the squid in this area. From one of their **vessels,** the scientists can see the great whales coming up to breathe. Sperm whales are huge **marine** creatures. They are eighty feet in length. They weigh up to sixty tons. Sperm whales can go without breathing for up to an hour. This lets them dive deep underwater. There they hunt for giant squid.

The giant squid is an enormous creature. Yet very few have been seen alive. Scientists instead **examine** dead squid that wash up on shore. The giant squid may grow to be sixty feet long when it is an adult. Its body is shaped like a **cylinder.** It has two fins at the tail end. It uses them for swimming. When it needs to, the squid can put on an extra burst of speed. First it swallows water. Then it shoots the water out through an opening in its tail. A **jet** of water rushes out. This pushes the giant squid forward.

The squid has two long, waving **tentacles.** Both are on its head. Each one has rows of hooks that can dig in deep. The squid uses them to grab food. It catches fish, crabs, and turtles. It also grabs smaller squid. It can capture anything else that swims within its reach. The squid also has eight arms. It uses them to stuff whatever it catches into its mouth. Then its powerful jaws go to work. Their jaws are shaped like a parrot's beak. Anything a giant squid **grasps** has little chance of getting away.

The most unusual **feature** of a squid is its eyes. They are the size of dinner plates. The squid lives far down in the ocean. There is only a small amount of light that deep. In the darkness, the squid's large eyes give it good eyesight. It can probably see a sperm whale before the whale comes close enough to attack. This helps the squid escape. Scientists have looked at **scars** on sperm whales. They believe the beaks of giant squid caused them. This tells them that a sperm whale's attack may not always be **fatal** for the giant squid.

The scientists use a small submarine to look for the squid. It is called a Deep Rover. This boat can dive to around 3,000 feet. It has powerful lights and four cameras. Scientists aboard a Deep Rover took the first pictures of a living giant squid. Scientists would love to one day film a fight between a whale and a giant squid. This is not very likely, however. Instead, what we may see on our television screens soon is the first close look at a giant squid. Its huge eyes will be staring at us out of the darkness.

Answer each of the questions with a sentence.

. . . .

1 Is it correct to call this a **marine** story? Explain your answer.

YES BECASE, OF tHE WATEр

2 What do the scientists aboard the submarine want to **examine?**

LIFE

3 How far down can the scientists' **vessel** travel?

3,000 FEEt

4 Why is it hard for sea creatures to escape the **grasp** of the giant squid?

TENTACALS HAVE SUCITN CUPS

cylinder
examine
fatal
feature
grasp
jet
marine
scar
tentacle
vessel

5 How does the **cylinder** shape of its body help a squid swim?

it HAS two FiNs For SWiMiNG

6 Why might a meeting with a sperm whale be **fatal** for a giant squid?

tHAY ArE NAthuL ENAMY'S

7 How do its **tentacles** help the giant squid?

to cAtch PhAY

8 Where does the **jet** of water come from that helps the giant squid move forward?

9 What do the **scars** on sperm whales tell scientists?

SQiuD ATACK's DUN DUhDUN...

10 Which **feature** of the giant squid seems most unusual to you?

NO FEAtupE it is BEUtiFALL

Fun
FACT

· ·

- You know **jet** as a fast stream of water and as an airplane.
  But there is also **jet** black, meaning a dark black color.
  That **jet** comes from the name of an ancient Greek town
  where a black stone, also called **jet,** was found. The two
  jets have no connection and are really two different words!

examine

verb To study or look at something closely.

Academic Context

In a science lesson, you might use a magnifying glass to **examine** an insect.

Word Family

exam (noun)

examination (noun)

Discussion & Writing Prompt

You could use a magnifying glass to **examine** a feather. What else could you **examine** using a magnifying glass?

2 min.	3 min.
1. Turn and talk to your partner or group.	**2.** Write 1–3 sentences.
Use this space to take notes or draw your ideas.	Be ready to share what you have written.

Study the words. Then do the exercises that follow.

attract

v. To bring or draw closer.

The large red flowers **attracted** both the hummingbird and Ming.

attractive *adj.* Pleasing to the eye or mind.

The bakery window, filled with pies, cakes, and cookies, was so **attractive** that Jean and I entered the shop.

attraction *n.* Something that draws attention.

One **attraction** Karen attends every September is the chowder festival near the dock.

 Pretend with your partner that your hands are magnets that are attracted to each other.

crew

n. A group of people working together, especially one that runs an airplane or large vessel.

The **crew** worked quickly to take down the sails on the boat before the storm hit.

dangle

v. To hang loosely.

Not yet ready to go into the pool, Ramona and Fernando sat by the edge and **dangled** their feet in the water.

 Show your partner how you dangle your legs from your chair.

drift

n. A pile of sand or snow created by moving air or water.

The **drifts** of snow in the driveway mean that we will all have to help with the shoveling.

v. To be carried along by moving air or water.

Liz climbed onto the rubber raft and let herself **drift** along the river for a while.

event

n. Something that happens, especially something important.

The big **event** of the week for Johnette and Derek was going to see *Swan Lake* with their aunt.

Discuss a special event with your partner.

launch

n. An open motorboat that is used for short distances.

The **launch** carried our class across the bay to one of the islands for a picnic.

v. 1. To put a boat or vessel in the water.

Leon and Greta **launched** the canoe onto the pond and started to paddle toward the other side.

2. To get something started.

Ms. Pinsky and Mr. Miller **launched** the clean-up day by giving everyone a pair of thick work gloves and some large plastic bags.

opposite

adj. 1. Very different from.

It is difficult to believe Ruth and Emily are sisters because they are **opposite** in so many ways.

2. Facing or moving away from each other.

After they got off the bus, Jorge and Janelle said good-bye and walked off in **opposite** directions.

Tell your partner what is the opposite of old.

reverse

v. To go backward or in the direction one just came from.

We laughed when Daniel suddenly **reversed** direction by walking backward.

adj. Back to front.

One side of this coin shows a head, and the **reverse** side shows a building.

signal

n. An object, action, or sound that gives a message or a warning.

Seeing the flashing red **signal,** Antonio told his brother they had to wait to cross the street.

v. To do something that gives a message or warning.

Jeff **signaled** the start of the race by dropping a white handkerchief.

. . . .

Signal your partner to be quiet.

steer

n. A young bull.

The herd of thirsty **steers** gathered near the stream.

v. To guide the direction of.

Bonnie carefully **steered** her bicycle around the rocks.

2A Using Words in Context

Read the sentences. If the word in bold is used correctly, write C on the line. If the word is used incorrectly, write I on the line.

❶ (a) Keisha tried to **dangle** her Mom into letting her have a sleepover. _____

(b) We sat on the dock and **dangled** our feet in the water. _____

(c) Neruda said her **dangle** was made of pure gold. _____

(d) We can get Bonzo excited just by **dangling** the dog leash. _____

2 (a) Her large floppy **crew** keeps the sun off her face. _____

(b) Tighten the **crew** to fix the wheel on the wagon. _____

(c) The vessel has a **crew** of six, not counting the skipper. _____

(d) I leave early with my **crew** when the grapes need to be picked. _____

3 (a) It's true that wasps are **attracted** to picnics. _____

(b) The roller coaster is the biggest **attraction** at the state fair. _____

(c) The most **attractive** part of town is next to the golf course. _____

(d) Juno tried to **attract** me into going with her to New York. _____

4 (a) Pick up the **launch** at the foot of your bed. _____

(b) A forty-foot **launch** is tied up at the dock next to ours. _____

(c) Marcus **launched** his new website yesterday. _____

(d) The vessel will be **launched** at noon tomorrow. _____

5 (a) You have to learn to **steer** the canoe with your paddle. _____

(b) My uncle **steered** me to the best amusement park in the state. _____

(c) The **steers** led to the second-floor bedroom. _____

(d) I was afraid that one of the **steers** might chase us. _____

6 (a) What Kumar told his parents was the **opposite** of the truth. _____

(b) Astronauts brought back pieces of **opposite** from the moon. _____

(c) Marsha lives on the **opposite** side of the street from me. _____

(d) The movie is completely **opposite** from the book. _____

7 (a) The **event** was found floating a mile out at sea. _____

(b) That book is an **event** I'll always remember. _____

(c) The next **event** at the club will be a rock concert. _____

(d) In the **event** I'm not home, just leave a note. _____

attract
crew
dangle
drift
event
launch
opposite
reverse
signal
steer

8 (a) The traffic cop **signaled** for me to stop. ____

(b) The Abraham Lincoln **signal** at the bottom of the letter was a fake. ____

(c) Not a **signal** person had a pencil for me to borrow. ____

(d) The firing of a cannon was the **signal** to start the boat race. ____

✓ 10/6

2B Making Connections

Circle the letter next to the correct answer.

1 Which word goes with *different from?*

(a) reverse (b) drift (c) same (d) steer

2 Which word goes with *birthday party?*

(a) event (b) marine (c) launch (d) signal

3 Which word goes with *teamwork?*

(a) drift (b) crew (c) steer (d) event

4 Which word goes with *boat on a river?*

(a) signal (b) cylinder (c) drift (d) event

5 Which word goes with *pretty?*

(a) attractive (b) reverse (c) fatal (d) marine

2C Using Context Clues

Circle the letter next to the word that correctly completes the sentence.

1 The last _____ on the program was the singing of the national anthem.

(a) diameter (b) steer (c) signal (d) event

2 The _____ of seven reports for work before daybreak.
(a) drift   (b) crew   (c) launch   (d) branch

3 East and west are _____ directions.
(a) opposite   (b) attractive   (c) marine   (d) fatal

4 The kitten _____ from José's arms when he picked it up.
(a) reversed   (b) drifted   (c) dangled   (d) signaled

5 A _____ is fully grown at two years of age.
(a) signal   (b) steer   (c) drift   (d) vessel

2D   Completing Sentences

Circle each answer choice that correctly completes the sentence. Each question has three correct answers.

1 The **launch**
(a) was one of the best meals I've had in my life.
(b) was big enough to hold twelve people.
(c) of the rocket was incredible.
(d) of such a large vessel takes careful planning.

2 **Drifts**
(a) happen when a boat puts down its anchor.
(b) of sand had formed on the pathway that led to the sea.
(c) of snow six feet high blocked the sidewalk.
(d) are caused by the wind blowing.

3 I **dangled**
(a) fifty feet above ground, holding on to the rope.
(b) the medal ribbon before him, daring him to snatch it.
(c) my legs over the side of the bridge.
(d) my way into the concert by saying I was with the band.

attract
crew
dangle
drift
event
launch
opposite
reverse
signal
steer

4 Reverse

(a) direction, and you start to go backward.

(b) the letters *x y z* and you get *z y x*.

(c) your way back through woods by following the signs.

(d) the dog gently on the nose to get its attention.

5 Signal

(a) the crowd when the game is about the start.

(b) that you're ready by saying, "I'm ready."

(c) what happened in your own words.

(d) the catcher that the next pitch is a fastball.

2E Vocabulary in Context
Read the passage.

Up, Up, and Away

Have you ever taken a ride in a hot-air balloon? It is exciting and gives those aboard a chance to see the world in a new way. A good place to learn about the sport is New Mexico. Let us go there. We'll explore the Albuquerque Balloon Fiesta.

• • • • • • • • • • • •

Almost a million people come to Albuquerque each October to see this colorful **event.** It lasts nine days. Over a thousand balloons take part. That is a fifth of all the hot-air balloons in the world.

Balloonists are **attracted** to this part of New Mexico for a special reason. The pilot of a hot-air balloon cannot **steer** it. It goes wherever the wind takes it. That is why most balloon trips end a long way from where they begin. In most places, a van with a **crew** of helpers follows the balloon. They keep it in view. When the balloon lands, the van is right there. It takes the passengers and the balloon back to the starting point.

In Albuquerque, it is different. An unusual wind pattern occurs there. It is called the "Albuquerque box." Winds from the Rio Grande valley pass over Albuquerque as they move east toward the

Sandia Mountains. But just a few hundred feet higher, a different wind blows toward the west. That makes Albuquerque a place where a round-trip balloon ride is possible.

The ride begins when the balloon is filled with hot air from a gas burner. Soon it rises in the air. The basket **dangles** beneath the balloon. Several helpers hold the basket down. Then the passengers climb inside. There is room for just three people plus the pilot.

When everything is ready, the pilot gives a **signal** to those on the ground: Let go! To the passengers, the balloon does not seem to be moving. The earth just looks like it is dropping away beneath them. The heat from the gas burner makes the balloon continue to rise. The burner is fixed in place above the basket; it blows hot air into the balloon through an opening at the bottom. When the balloon reaches the right height, the pilot turns down the gas burner.

Passengers enjoy wonderful views in all directions. They see the houses and streets of Albuquerque the way a thousand-foot giant would. Cars look like little toys. People seem no bigger than ants. They are surprised by how quiet the ride is. The air is perfectly still. The balloon just **drifts** with the wind.

After about thirty minutes, it is time to **reverse** the direction of the balloon. The pilot turns up the heat. Again the balloon rises. The wind at the higher level is blowing in the **opposite** direction. The balloon is now heading back toward Albuquerque. As it gets closer to the starting point, the pilot turns down the gas burner. The balloon sinks slowly. It lands with a gentle bump. The ride is over.

The Albuquerque Balloon Fiesta is an exciting time even for those who stay on the ground. The high point is the **launching** of hundreds of balloons from Fiesta Park. The launch takes place in the space of an hour. The balloons come in many colors. They fill the whole sky. Some have unusual shapes. Visitors might see a cow, a teddy bear, or a pink dragon floating overhead. Balloonists are serious about their sport. But they also like to have fun.

attract
crew
dangle
drift
event
launch
opposite
reverse
signal
steer

Answer each of the questions with a sentence.

1. What would be the most exciting **attraction** for you at the Balloon Fiesta?

   _____

   _____

2. How do you know that two balloons going in **opposite** directions near Albuquerque will not run into each other?

   _____

   _____

3. How is the work different for the **crew** in Albuquerque compared to other places?

   _____

   _____

4. What happens when it is time to **launch** the hot-air balloon?

   _____

   _____

5. If you were the pilot, how could you **signal** to the crew on the ground?

   _____

   _____

6. What do you think you would enjoy most about **drifting** along in a hot-air balloon?

   _____

   _____

7. How can a pilot **reverse** the direction of a balloon that is rising?

   _____

   _____

8 How does a pilot **steer** a hot-air balloon?

_____

_____

9 What **dangles** under a hot-air balloon?

_____

_____

10 Why is the Albuquerque Fiesta a special **event** for people with hot-air balloons?

_____

_____

Fun FACT

• •

- You may have heard of the hairstyle known as the **crew** cut. This haircut, buzzed very short on the sides and flat on the top, began with teams, or **crews**, of racing-boat rowers. All the rowers cut their hair in the same way to create team spirit. After a time, the hairstyle became known as the "crew cut" whether the person wearing it was a rower or not.

attract
crew
dangle
drift
event
launch
opposite
reverse
signal
steer

reverse

verb To go backward or in the direction one just came from.

adjective The opposite side of something.

Word Family

reversal (noun)

reversible (adjective)

Context Clues

These sentences give clues to the meaning of **reverse.**

*Marco's dad **reversed** the car into the parking space.*

*The name of Lydia's softball team is on the front side of her jersey, and her number is on the **reverse** side.*

Discussion & Writing Prompt

How would you make a toy car go in the **reverse** direction?

2 min.	3 min.
1. Turn and talk to your partner or group.	2. Write 1–3 sentences.
Use this space to take notes or draw your ideas.	Be ready to share what you have written.

Review

Hidden Message Write the word that is missing from each sentence in the boxes next to it. All the words are from Lessons 1 and 2. The shaded boxes will answer the following riddle:

Cowboy Tex rode into town on Friday. He stayed two days and left on Friday. How can that be?

1. The rocket _____ was scheduled for 8:00 a.m.

2. The jeweler bent close to _____ the diamond.

3. Maria's knee was badly scraped, but the doctor said there would not be a(n) _____.

4. People think I am smart, but I often feel just the _____.

5. The boat started to _____ away, but we caught it in time.

6. As if on a given _____, all the birds started singing at once.

7. My grandmother called my baby brother's birth a "blessed _____."

8. The giant squid's long _____ broke the surface of the water.

9. My favorite flowers are the ones that _____ bees.

10. Tony wanted to live near the ocean and study _____ life.

11. We waited on the airstrip while the _____ checked the plane.

12. Everyone cheered as our team's running back broke free of the tackler's _____.

13. Sailors lined the ship's deck, waiting for their _____ to dock.

14. The bite of certain snakes can be _____.

15. Jonah sat back and let me _____ the boat.

16. We crawled through a big _____ at the playground.

17. Ben liked to tease his dog and _____ chew toys in his face.

18. The most important _____ of the statue was the head, which was realistic.

Study the words. Then do the exercises that follow.

ambition

n. A strong wish to be good at something or to have something.

Clare's **ambition** was to dive into the pool without making a splash.

 Tell your partner about an ambition you have.

auction

n. A public sale. Each item is sold to the person who offers the most money.

At the **auction,** Peter's uncle bought a maple desk.

coast

n. The land beside the sea.

After we reached the **coast,** we walked a long way on the beach.

v. To move without power or effort.

Gabriella and Lucy quickly pedaled their bikes to the top of the hill and then **coasted** down the other side.

 Describe to your partner what it might feel like to coast down a steep hill.

current

n. A flow of air, water, or electricity.

The lifeguard told us not to swim to the middle of the river, because the **current** there was very strong.

adj. Of the present time.

Is Caroline's **current** address 7 Elm Street, or did she move?

frail

adj. Weak, not very strong.

Danny looked **frail** when I visited him in the hospital after his operation.

intelligent

adj. Able to learn, think, and understand quickly and easily.

In our science book, we are reading some stories that show how **intelligent** dolphins are.

novel

n. A long story about people and events that are imagined by the author.

Have you read any **novels** by Laura Ingalls Wilder?

adj. New and different.

In 1990, the Internet was a **novel** way to find information.

Demonstrate for your partner a novel way to walk.

resident

n. A person who lives in a certain place.

May we go to this beach to swim, or is it for the **residents** of the town only?

Talk with your partner about how many residents you think your town has.

starve

v. To be very hungry or to suffer because of not eating any food.

The farmers want to bring hay to the animals trapped by the flood before they **starve.**

volunteer

> *n.* A person who offers to do a job, usually without pay.
>
> Marco, who is a **volunteer** in our class, helps Mrs. Stevens with the art projects.
>
> *v.* To choose to do something or to give help.
>
> Cathy **volunteered** to help in the library on Thursday mornings.

· ·

Discuss with your partner what you could volunteer to do to help your teacher.

3A Words and Their Meanings

Look at the group of words next to the number. Then circle the letter next to the word that has the same meaning.

1 someone who lives in a place

(a) auction   (b) coast   (c) current   (d) resident

2 a sale to the person paying the most

(a) volunteer   (b) novel   (c) auction   (d) ambition

3 taking place now

(a) current   (b) intelligent   (c) novel   (d) frail

4 a wish to be very good at something

(a) novel   (b) ambition   (c) coast   (d) volunteer

5 able to understand quickly

(a) frail   (b) novel   (c) intelligent   (d) coast

Look at the word next to the number. Then circle the letter next to the group of words that has the same meaning.

6 volunteer

(a) offer to help   (b) change direction

(c) turn away   (d) look closely

7 coast

(a) stop without warning   (b) reverse position

(c) move without using effort (d) return to starting place

8 starve

(a) put money away   (b) be without food for a long time

(c) waste time   (d) be without sleep for a long time

9 novel

(a) kind and gentle   (b) timid and quiet

(c) slow and painful   (d) new and unusual

10 frail

(a) not easy   (b) not nice

(c) not strong   (d) not open

ambition
auction
coast
current
frail
intelligent
novel
resident
starve
volunteer

Just the Right Word

Replace each phrase in bold with a single word (or form of the word) from the word list.

1. One of our favorite vacation spots is the **land beside the sea.**

2. Your pet will **be very hungry** if you fail to give it food.

3. The hospital relied on **people who do a job without pay** to cheer up patients.

4. Her **strong wish to be good at something** made her spend hours at practice.

5. This gadget measures the **flow of electricity** in volts.

Applying Meanings

Circle the letter next to the correct answer.

1. Which of the following can help you become more **intelligent?**
   (a) eating
   (b) sleeping
   (c) reading
   (d) forgetting

2. Which of the following can **coast?**
   (a) a flagpole
   (b) a bicycle
   (c) a sandwich
   (d) a horse

3. Which of the following might be a person's **ambition?**
   (a) to pack a lunch
   (b) to take a nap
   (c) to water the plants
   (d) to climb mountains

4. Which of the following could cause animals to **starve?**
   (a) not enough food
   (b) not enough water
   (c) too much heat
   (d) too much exercise

5 When are you most likely to be **frail?**

    (a) when you are exercising   (b) when you are reading

    (c) when you are eating   (d) when you are sick

Word Study: Adjectives

An adjective tells about something and gives details. Underline the adjectives in the sentences.

1 My current favorite book is about baby animals.

2 A kitten has a frail voice that is hard to hear when it cries.

3 Did you know that pigs are one of the most intelligent animals?

4 Training monkeys to help people who can't walk is a novel idea.

5 Monkeys can learn to bring a book from the opposite end of a room to a person in a wheelchair.

Vocabulary in Context

Read the passage.

ambition
auction
coast
current
frail
intelligent
novel
resident
starve
volunteer

Roundup Time in Virginia

You might think cowboys round up wild horses only in the movies. But there is an island near Virginia where this really happens. Let us explore Assateague [as-sa-teeg] Island and learn about its famous wild horses.

· · · · · · · · · · · · ·

What are wild horses doing there? Some say they first arrived on the island in the 1500s, when a Spanish ship was wrecked in the Atlantic Ocean. The horses on board swam ashore. Others say that is just a story. We know this for certain: The horses have been on the island for hundreds of years. There are no **residents** on the island. The horses have it all to themselves.

Assateague horses do not grow very big. Most are the size of a pony. Perhaps that is because there are not many kinds of plants to eat on the island. The horses live mostly on marsh grass, which is quite salty. They also feed on seaweed. They even eat poison ivy. Assateague horses take in a lot of salt. This causes them to drink twice as much water as other horses. All that water makes them look rather fat around the middle.

The island of Assateague is not very big. Sometimes the number of horses grows too large for the island. Then there is not enough grass for all of the animals. Some of them could **starve.** The people on the nearby island of Chincoteague [shin-ka-teeg] came up with an idea to help the horses. Chincoteague lies between Assateague and the Virginia **coast.** Its firefighters, who are all **volunteers,** hold a summer roundup of the horses and then sell them. This helps to control the number of horses. It also raises money for their fire department.

The firefighters go to Assateague. They collect as many of the horses as they can. A vet then examines each one to make sure they are healthy. Those that are too young or too **frail** stay on the island. The rest of the horses are driven into the water. They have to swim across the narrow channel to Chincoteague. It is only about a hundred yards away. The roundup usually takes place on the last Wednesday of July. That's when the sea is calm and the **current** is not strong.

First the horses swim ashore. They spend the night penned up in the center of the town. The next day there is an **auction.** Up to eighty animals might be sold. Some do not sell. They swim back to Assateague to wait for another year. Usually, people pay about two thousand dollars for one of the horses. The new owners like these animals. They are **intelligent** and easy to train. Young children enjoy riding them because of their small size.

Many people first heard of these creatures by reading a **novel** by Marguerite Henry. The book is called *Misty of Chincoteague*. It came out in 1947. It tells the story of Paul and Maureen Beebe, two children who have one great **ambition.** They want to own one of the wild horses that run free on Assateague. You can discover how they find Misty, the horse of their dreams. And you can learn how they get the money to buy her. All you have to do is read the book!

Answer each of the questions with a sentence.

1 What details tell how the people of Chincoteague have succeeded in their **ambition** to keep the wild horses from going hungry?

_____

_____

2 Why would the new owners be happy to have an **intelligent** horse?

_____

_____

3 What **novel** idea did the people of Chincoteague have for controlling the number of wild horses?

_____

_____

4 What do you know about the **residents** of Assateague Island?

_____

_____

5 What might cause the wild horses on Assateague to **starve?**

_____

_____

6 In which ocean off the Virginia **coast** might a Spanish ship have wrecked in the 1500s?

_____

_____

| ambition |
| auction |
| coast |
| current |
| frail |
| intelligent |
| novel |
| resident |
| starve |
| volunteer |

7 Which people **volunteer** to take part in the summer roundup?

_____

_____

8 How are **frail** horses kept back from the sale?

_____

_____

9 Why are the horses not swept away by a strong **current** as they swim?

_____

_____

10 How is the money from the **auction** used?

_____

_____

Fun
FACT

· ·

• The words **current** and **currant** sound the same but have different spellings and meanings. They are homophones. A **currant** is a type of berry. It is also a type of seedless raisin.

Vocabulary Extension

intelligent

adjective Able to learn, think, and understand quickly and easily.

Some types of dogs are easy to train because they are **intelligent.**

Word Family

intelligence (noun)
intelligently (adverb)

Synonyms

smart, bright, clever

Discussion & Writing Prompt

Ali speaks **intelligently** *about model airplanes. He knows how to build them, fix them, and fly them.*

After reading these sentences, what do you think **intelligently** means?

2 min.	3 min.
1. Turn and talk to your partner or group.	**2.** Write 1–3 sentences.
Use this space to take notes or draw your ideas.	Be ready to share what you have written.

Study the words. Then do the exercises that follow.

average

n. 1. The usual amount or kind of something.

Twenty students in a class is the **average** for Edison School.

2. The result of adding a set of numbers and then dividing the total by the number in the set.

The **average** of 2, 3, and 7 is 4.

adj. Not special or unusual; ordinary.

Mr. Barnes, who is just over 7 feet tall, is not of **average** height.

 Tell your partner something about you that is average.

border

n. 1. A dividing line between two states or countries.

The Niagara River marks the **border** between Canada and the United States.

2. The edge of something.

The old tablecloth had a **border** of fine lace.

v. To be next to.

The United States **borders** Mexico to the south and Canada to the north.

 Show your partner how you can draw a special border around a piece of paper.

cocoon

n. The silky case that a caterpillar makes to protect itself for a time before it becomes a moth.

The empty **cocoon** hanging from the leaf meant the moth had already flown away.

flutter

v. To wave or flap quickly.

Sitting by their clubhouse, Olivia and Victor watched their flag **flutter** above them.

moisture

n. A small amount of liquid, often in the form of small drops.

Carla sat on the bench and wiped the **moisture** from her face with a towel.

moist *adj.* Damp or slightly wet.

Grass snakes usually live in **moist** places like the banks of rivers.

nectar

n. A sweet liquid produced by many flowering plants. It is used by bees to make honey.

The bees hummed among the flowers of the cherry tree as they gathered **nectar**.

process

n. A number of steps that one takes in order to do or make something.

In early spring, Uncle Ted and Aunt Flora began the **process** of making maple syrup by collecting sap from their maple trees.

Talk to your partner about your process for getting ready for school.

span

> *n.* 1. The distance or a section between two objects or supports.
>
> The bridge at Cape Girardeau, Missouri, has three **spans**.
>
> 2. A period or length of time.
>
> With a life **span** of seventeen years, the cicada is probably the longest-living insect.
>
> *v.* To stretch from one side to the other.
>
> The Harahan Bridge, which **spans** the Mississippi River between Tennessee and Arkansas, is over one hundred years old.

> *Show your partner how you can make a pencil span from one hand to the other.*

suitable

> *adj.* Fit or right for some purpose or event.
>
> Checkers and other games with small parts are not **suitable** for very young children, who might try to swallow the pieces.

> *Discuss with your partner foods you think are suitable for breakfast.*

timber

> *n.* 1. Wooded areas with trees that can be used for wood products.
>
> The piece of land next to Jackson's farm was sold for its **timber**.
>
> 2. Tree trunks that can be cut into planks or boards.
>
> As we drove down the mountain, we followed a truck loaded with **timber** on its way to a sawmill.

4A

Using Words in Context

Read the sentences. If the word in bold is used correctly, write C on the line. If the word is used incorrectly, write I on the line.

1 (a) **Timber,** in the form of logs, is floated down the coast to Seattle. _____

(b) The bricks were made out of stone **timber.** _____

(c) Each **timber** dropped softly from the sky like a feather. _____

(d) These giant redwoods are protected and cannot be used for **timber.** _____

2 (a) Damon studied the **process** of becoming a U.S. citizen for homework. _____

(b) The sound of **process** filled her ears. _____

(c) Each step in the **process** takes time and money. _____

(d) Aunt Sal says that the **process** for making jam starts with washing the fruit. _____

3 (a) Bees are attracted to flowers that produce **nectar.** _____

(b) The love of a friend is sweeter than **nectar.** _____

(c) **Nectar** can be found deep underground. _____

(d) Jeremiah likes to pour **nectar** on his cereal. _____

average
border
cocoon
flutter
moisture
nectar
process
span
suitable
timber

4 (a) The life **span** of a mayfly is about twenty-four hours. _____

(b) New York's Brooklyn Bridge **spans** the East River. _____

(c) The spider **span** its web while we sat and watched it. _____

(d) The novel **spans** the years from the Civil War to World War II. _____

5 (a) Take a **moist** cloth and wipe the child's face. _____

(b) The hose puts **moisture** into the air. _____

(c) The **moisture** in the room was at least an inch thick. _____

(d) Put the jar of **moisture** back on the shelf. _____

6 (a) Maria **fluttered** her eyelashes and smiled. ____

(b) The **fluttering** of the curtain was caused by the breeze. ____

(c) We watched the butterflies **flutter** around the tall grass. ____

(d) The fog **fluttered** a few feet above the ground. ____

7 (a) The U.S. is **bordered** by Canada and Mexico. ____

(b) The cotton tablecloth had a four-inch painted **border.** ____

(c) The moon moves around the Earth in a fixed **border.** ____

(d) The **border** between Mexico and the U.S. is 2,000 miles long. ____

8 (a) The **average** height of the Washington Monument is 555 feet. ____

(b) An **average** ball player will not make it to the NBA. ____

(c) There are twelve inches to a foot on **average.** ____

(d) The **average** age of the class is eight years and six months. ____

4B Making Connections
Circle the letter next to the correct answer.

1 Which word goes with *caterpillar?*

(a) moisture (b) flutter (c) cocoon (d) nectar

2 Which word goes with *just right?*

(a) average (b) current (c) novel (d) suitable

3 Which word goes with *bridge?*

(a) span (b) utensil (c) border (d) nectar

4 Which word goes with *ordinary?*

(a) process (b) average (c) current (d) intelligent

5 Which word goes with *edge?*
(a) average   (b) border   (c) cocoon   (d) volunteer

6 Which word goes with *trees?*
(a) nectar   (b) auction   (c) coast   (d) timber

7 Which word goes with *wet?*
(a) moisture   (b) cocoon   (c) resident   (d) process

8 Which word goes with *butterfly?*
(a) starve   (b) flutter   (c) timber   (d) span

4C Using Context Clues

Circle the letter next to the word that correctly completes the sentence.

1 Janeen's eyes grew _____ whenever she thought of home.
(a) frail   (b) moist   (c) features   (d) scars

2 The _____ is cut into boards two inches thick.
(a) cocoon   (b) span   (c) moisture   (d) timber

3 This looks like the _____ of a monarch butterfly.
(a) flutter   (b) resident   (c) border   (d) cocoon

4 I was just a(n) _____ player, but I still made the team.
(a) suitable   (b) frail   (c) average   (d) reverse

5 Bees turn the _____ into honey.
(a) nectar   (b) timber   (c) cylinder   (d) moisture

average
border
cocoon
flutter
moisture
nectar
process
span
suitable
timber

6 The _____ begins with the first step.

(a) current   (b) volunteer   (c) process   (d) average

7 Choose a book that is _____ for someone her age.

(a) average   (b) current   (c) fatal   (d) suitable

4D Completing Sentences

Circle each answer choice that correctly completes the sentence. Each question has three correct answers.

1 Madame Chu is looking for a **suitable**

(a) school for her young son.

(b) birthday present for a six-year-old.

(c) name for her new launch.

(d) span of five years.

2 The **process**

(a) is heated in an oven to over one thousand degrees.

(b) is listed in an easy-to-follow way.

(c) will be hard to stop once it has begun.

(d) that we have decided on is not safe.

3 The **fluttering**

(a) of the butterfly's wings grabbed my attention.

(b) of the national flag makes me feel proud.

(c) could be heard for miles around.

(d) movement was caused by the light breeze.

4 A **border** can be

(a) the edge of something.

(b) a dividing line between two states.

(c) the difference between two numbers.

(d) a pattern around the outside of a blanket.

5 **Nectar**

(a) is made by mixing orange and lemon juice.

(b) is what draws bees to certain flowers.

(c) is a sweet liquid.

(d) is made into honey inside a bee hive.

Vocabulary in Context
Read the passage.

Monarchs of the Air

Butterflies are some of nature's prettiest creatures. Monarch butterflies are especially attractive. They are a common sight in many parts of North America during the summer. You may have seen them floating lightly on the air. It is hard to believe they make flights of up to 2,000 miles. But they do. So let's discover where these butterflies go for the winter.

• • • • • • • • • • • • • •

Monarch butterflies set out from the northern states and Canada. That's where they spend the summer. They leave in late August through October. Those that live west of the Rocky Mountains fly further west. They head for the California coast. Those east of the Rockies travel south. They head for the fir trees of the mountains of central Mexico. Monarch butterflies like Mexico. It is cold but not freezing. It also has the right amount of **moisture** in the air. Hundreds of millions of monarchs gather in one small area. They completely cover the trees. They stay there through the winter months. During that time they barely move.

average
border
cocoon
flutter
moisture
nectar
process
span
suitable
timber

By the middle of March, it is time for them to head north again. During their return flight, female monarch butterflies land in different patches of milkweed. They lay their eggs on the underside of the leaves. Soon after, the females die. A week or so passes. Then tiny caterpillars come out of the eggs. They start feeding on the milkweed. Its leaves have a poison. That poison stays inside the caterpillars and adult butterflies. It does not hurt them, though. Instead, it is harmful to the birds that eat them. After becoming sick, the birds learn from their mistake. Next time they choose other creatures for food.

When the caterpillars are fully grown, they stop eating. Each makes a chrysalis around itself. This is a pouch sort of like a moth's **cocoon.** Now they can begin the **process** of changing into a butterfly. After about two weeks, they break out of these pouches. They unfold and stretch their wings. Then they are ready to continue the flight north, which their parents had begun. How do they know where to go? It is a big mystery. But they keep flying and flying. Finally they arrive. They are at the very places their parents left in late summer.

The butterflies that flew south for the winter had a life **span** of five or six months. But the summer butterflies live an **average** of only four weeks. In this short time, they feed on the **nectar** of lilacs and other flowers. Then they lay their eggs and die. This cycle is repeated. It takes place three, four, or five times over the summer. The butterflies that go south in the fall are probably the great-great-grandchildren of those that arrived in the spring. They too will live for about six months.

Sadly, there are fewer and fewer places where monarch butterflies can spend the winter months. In central Mexico, the forests are being cut down for **timber.** In California, the trees along the coast continue to be cleared. Houses and shopping malls are built in their place. The result is fewer **suitable** wintering places for the monarch butterflies. Adding to their troubles is the need of farmers in the United States and Canada to get rid of milkweed. To them it is a weed. Not to the monarch butterflies, though. It is the only food their caterpillars can eat.

You might be able to attract monarch butterflies to your area. Try planting clumps of milkweed in sunny areas sheltered from the wind. They may reward you with a visit. They are easy to spot. They have large orange wings about four inches across. The wings have black **borders** and white markings. As you watch them **flutter** by, think about the long journey that they will soon make.

Answer each of the following questions with a sentence. If a question does not contain a vocabulary word from the lesson's word list, use one in your answer. Use each word only once.

1 What does an empty chrysalis or **cocoon** tell you?

_____

_____

2 What do monarch butterflies feed on?

_____

_____

3 How far across are the wings of a monarch butterfly?

_____

_____

4 On **average,** how many times are new groups of monarch butterflies born in the summer?

_____

_____

5 When would a butterfly's wings not **flutter?**

_____

_____

average
border
cocoon
flutter
moisture
nectar
process
span
suitable
timber

6 How many times would a monarch butterfly cross the **border** of a country on its journey from Canada to Mexico?

_____

_____

7 What kind of place do monarch butterflies need for their winter resting place?

_____

_____

8 How long does it take the caterpillar to turn into a monarch butterfly?

_____

_____

9 Is milkweed a **suitable** food for birds? Explain your answer.

_____

_____

10 If the forests in central Mexico are used for **timber,** what do you think will happen to the monarch butterflies?

_____

_____

Fun FACT

- In stories about Greek gods and goddesses, we read how they often enjoyed their favorite drink, a liquid called **nectar.** We do not know what it tasted like, but we do know it was different from the liquid produced by flowers.

process

noun A set of steps that a person follows in order to do or make something.

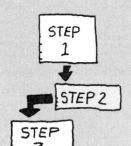

. . . .

Academic Context

In school, you learn the **process** for doing things, such as making artwork.

Other Usages

in the process of In the middle of doing something; having started but not finished.

> Mom was **in the process of** *making dinner when the doorbell rang.*

Discussion & Writing Prompt

Make a list that shows the **process** you follow when you arrive at school each day.

2 min.	3 min.
1. Turn and talk to your partner or group.	**2.** Write 1–3 sentences.
Use this space to take notes or draw your ideas.	Be ready to share what you have written.

Review

Lessons 3 & 4

Crossword Puzzle Solve the puzzle by writing the missing word in each sentence in the boxes with the matching numbers. All the words are from Lessons 3 and 4.

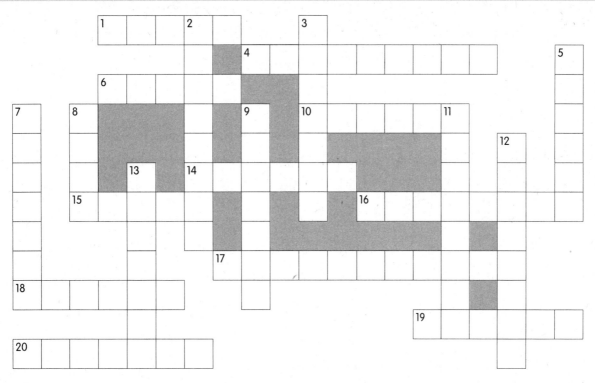

ACROSS

1. The _____ of Jamaica boasts fine beaches.

4. We need another _____ for the school play.

6. The baby elephant seemed so wobbly and _____ when it stood up.

10. Oak Forest is our region's source of _____ .

14. The police officers asked us where we lived when we drove across the _____.

15. After I finish my homework, I will begin the new _____ by my favorite author.

16. Chan's _____ for summer is to learn to swim.

17. Watch this trick! See how _____ our dog is!

18. How happy bees must be when they land on the flowers with sweet _____!

19. If koalas don't eat leaves, they'll _____.

20. Follow this _____ exactly to bake the cake.

DOWN

2. The zoo's small, crowded area was not _____ for the lions.

3. The flags outside the school building began to _____ as the wind increased.

5. On cold winter nights, Emma imagined herself as a moth in a cozy _____.

7. We will have a(n) _____ to sell all the old furniture.

8. Lydia's team has won three championships over a(n) _____ of five years.

9. What is your _____ favorite song?

11. Last year, Sheila became a(n) _____ of Florida.

12. There was so much rain that _____ was seeping through our walls.

13. I am not a great baseball player, just a(n) _____ one.

Study the words. Then do the exercises that follow.

amaze

v. To surprise or cause wonder.

Freddy **amazed** his parents by tidying his room without being told.

amazing *adj.* Causing wonder or surprise.

It is **amazing** but true that time would slow down aboard a spaceship traveling at very high speed.

 Tell your partner about something you have seen that was amazing.

arctic

adj. Very cold.

Many people could not start their cars during last week's **arctic** weather.

Arctic *n.* The area around the North Pole.

Polar bears, caribou, and snowy owls are some of the animals that live in the **Arctic.**

court

n. 1. An open, flat area marked off for a game or sport.

After school, my friends and I met at the basketball **court** to practice different shots.

2. The home of a king, queen, or other royal person.

Each spring, knights and ladies gathered at the **court** of Queen Eleanor of France for contests, food, and dance.

3. The place where a judge holds trials and decides matters of law.

Everyone stood when Judge Jurgen entered the **court** and took her place on the bench.

 Talk with your partner about what a judge might say or do in court.

elect

v. 1. To choose by voting for.

The fourth-grade students **elected** Jill the class president.

2. To make a choice.

This year Sui Lu **elected** to go to a summer camp closer to home.

· ·

Tell your partner what you will elect to do at recess today.

interval

n. 1. A period of time between events.

The announcer explained that there would be a ten-minute **interval** before the next race began.

2. A space between two things.

The row of old oak trees, bordering the road, had been planted at **intervals** of forty feet.

· ·

Discuss with your partner how long the interval is between breakfast and lunch.

league

n. 1. A group of people that works together for a common purpose.

The **league** began in 1993 to protect the wild lands in Alaska.

2. A group of sports teams that play each other to see which is best.

Third baseman Ellis has the best batting average in our **league.**

limit

n. A line or point beyond which one may not go.

At our library, the **limit** to the number of books a person can borrow at one time is ten.

v. To keep from going beyond a certain point.

Because the party will be in the park, we will not **limit** the number of people who can attend.

Tell your partner why there should or should not be a limit to how late you can stay at a friend's house.

milestone

n. 1. A stone marker that gives the distance in miles to another point.

On our hike, we rested by a **milestone** that said "Camden 26 miles."

2. An important event.

Sending humans to the moon and bringing them back to Earth was an important **milestone** in the history of space travel.

recreation

n. Anything a person does to relax or have fun; play.

Sanaa's favorite **recreation** is ice-skating.

tackle

v. 1. To grab or get in the way of a player in a game to stop the player or take the ball away.

Just as I caught the ball, Ian **tackled** me.

2. To do or try to do something.

Dad told my brother and me that after cleaning our rooms, we could **tackle** the basement.

n. The tools needed for some activity or sport.

Opening the box of fishing **tackle,** we found hooks, lines, weights, and floats.

Words and Their Meanings

Look at the group of words next to the number. Then circle the letter next to the word that has the same meaning.

1 to select by voting
(a) tackle   (b) limit   (c) amaze   (d) elect

2 some space between two things
(a) interval   (b) league   (c) limit   (d) court

3 an important event
(a) recreation   (b) court   (c) milestone   (d) league

4 the tools used for a certain sport
(a) limit   (b) tackle   (c) league   (d) recreation

Look at the word next to the number. Then circle the letter next to the group of words that has the same meaning.

5 recreation
(a) something done for money   (b) something done to help others
(c) something done for fun   (d) something that takes skill

6 arctic
(a) very hungry   (b) very cold
(c) very sorry   (d) very tired

7 court
(a) a home for a king or queen   (b) the home of an animal
(c) the home of a judge   (d) a home without a basement

8 amaze
(a) to keep from going further   (b) to keep a careful record of
(c) to cause surprise   (d) to avoid or stay away from

Just the Right Word

Replace each phrase in bold with a single word (or form of the word) from the word list.

1 The hospital **keeps control of** the number of visitors each patient can have at one time.

2 You must be between twelve and eighteen years old to play tennis in this **group of sports teams that play against each other.**

3 The **area around the North Pole** is actually a frozen sea.

4 The **stone marker that said how far it was to the next town** was hard to read because it was old and beginning to crumble.

5 This Saturday I want you to **make the effort to do** the leaves in the backyard.

6 The **place where matters of law are decided** is closed on Monday for the Memorial Day holiday.

7 Those who **decide that they would like** to go on Saturday to the history museum must bring a signed note from a parent.

8 There was a short **period of time** between the two movies so that people could stand up and stretch.

amaze
arctic
court
elect
interval
league
limit
milestone
recreation
tackle

Circle the letter next to the correct answer.

1 Which of the following could you see in the **Arctic?**

(a) polar bears

(b) pineapple trees

(c) tigers

(d) rattlesnakes

2 Why might someone join a **league?**

(a) to eat at a restaurant

(b) to play a sport

(c) to sleep comfortably

(d) to read a book

3 Which of the following would be an **amazing** event?

(a) watching a sailboat race

(b) falling overboard while sailing

(c) losing an oar while rowing

(d) crossing the ocean in a rowboat

4 When would you be on a **court?**

(a) while taking a shower

(b) while hiking in the mountains

(c) while playing basketball

(d) while watching television

5 Which of the following might people do for **recreation?**

(a) clean their bedroom

(b) go to the beach

(c) go to school

(d) eat lunch

6 Where could you find a **milestone?**

(a) in a book on space history

(b) at a hardware store

(c) in a coal mine

(d) in the refrigerator

7 Which person do you **tackle?**

(a) a golfer

(b) a runner

(c) a football player

(d) a swimmer

8 What is the **limit** of the sky?

(a) ten miles

(b) ten thousand miles

(c) one thousand miles

(d) there is not any

5D Word Study: Parts of Speech

Read the sentence and decide which part of speech the bold word is. Write its part of speech—noun, verb, or adjective—on the line.

Sometimes there is no way to tell which part of speech a word is just by looking at it. The only way to know whether it is a noun, a verb, or an adjective is to look at how the word is used in the sentence. Here are five examples:

average   border   limit   span   tackle

1 The **average** age of the members of my class is nine and a half years. _____

2 The **average** of the different times was exactly seven minutes. _____

3 Jonah decided to **limit** himself to one ice-cream cone a week. _____

4 The speed **limit** on this stretch of road is 40 miles per hour. _____

5 The life **span** of the mayfly is measured in just hours. _____

6 The new railroad being built will **span** the country from sea to sea. _____

7 The fishing **tackle** is kept in a small plastic box. _____

8 We decided to **tackle** the problem head on. _____

9 The Mississippi River runs along the **border** between Missouri and Illinois. _____

10 To ask fifty dollars for that old bike really does **border** on the ridiculous. _____

amaze
arctic
court
elect
interval
league
limit
milestone
recreation
tackle

Hoop, Hoop, Hurray!

Mention basketball, and a few names come to mind. One name might be Larry Bird, or Michael Jordan, or LeBron James. But did you ever hear of James Naismith? Here is a clue. The full name of the basketball museum in Springfield, Massachusetts, is the Naismith Memorial Basketball Hall of Fame. Let's discover who James Naismith was. Why is his name the first in the history of basketball?

In 1891, Naismith was teaching physical education at a college in Springfield. The director of the department was Luther Gulick. He was looking for a new kind of **recreation** during the winter months for the young men at the school. New England's **arctic** weather made outdoor games impossible. Students found indoor exercises boring. Gulick wanted a game that could be played within the **limits** of their indoor space.

Naismith went to work at once. He decided that skill at handling and throwing the ball, not speed or strength, was what the game needed. The goals should be above the players' heads at each end of the playing area. Then only a curving shot would score. Nine players on each side seemed the right number. Soon Naismith had drawn up thirteen rules listing what could and could not be done during the game. A player could score from anywhere on the **court.** There was to be no running with the ball and no **tackling.** There would be two periods of play, each lasting fifteen minutes. There would be only one **interval,** or break.

Luther Gulick liked Naismith's idea. On December 21, 1891, the world's first basketball game took place. But it still did not have a name. By chance, the person who helped name the game was the school janitor. Naismith had asked him for two wooden boxes to use as goals. There were no boxes of the right size. Instead, the janitor found two peach baskets. These worked well for the goals. One of the players, Frank Mahan, suggested that the game be called

Naismithball. With a name like that, Naismith replied, the game would never catch on. Then Mahan thought of the peach-basket goals. "Basketball," he said. And so it was.

The new game quickly became popular. The first national basketball **league** was formed in 1898. It had six teams. There were other important **milestones** in the game's history. In 1936, basketball first became an Olympic event. That year, the United States team won the gold. In 1947, wheelchair basketball began. Today, basketball is played in almost every country in the world.

The best record in basketball belongs to the Edmonton Grads. They were an **amazing** women's team from Canada. They played 522 games from 1915 to 1940. The team won all but twenty of them. James Naismith said of them, "They are the finest team that ever stepped on the floor." Curiously, Naismith, who died in 1939, played in only two basketball games. The first was in 1892 and the second in 1898. When asked why he had played so rarely, he replied, "I just never got around to it." James Naismith was **elected** to basketball's hall of fame in 1959.

Answer each of the following questions with a sentence. If a question does not contain a vocabulary word from the lesson's word list, use one in your answer. Use each word only once.

. . . .

1 What job did Naismith **tackle** in 1891?

_____

_____

2 Describe the playing area Naismith set up for basketball.

_____

_____

3 What **limit** was placed on the length of the game?

_____

_____

amaze
arctic
court
elect
interval
league
limit
milestone
recreation
tackle

4 Why is December 21, 1891, a **milestone** in the history of sports?

_____

_____

5 Against which other teams would a wheelchair basketball team play?

_____

_____

6 Why do you think Naismith was **elected** to the Basketball Hall of Fame even though he did not play the game?

_____

_____

7 How did the New England weather help create the game of basketball?

_____

_____

8 Name two other forms of **recreation** besides basketball that have two teams playing against each other.

_____

_____

9 How many breaks are there in a game that is made up of four quarters?

_____

_____

10 Do you think it is **amazing** that James Naismith, who invented basketball, played in only two games? Explain your answer.

_____

_____

Fun FACT

● The area around the South Pole is opposite to the **Arctic** and is called the *Antarctic*. Both the North and South Poles are very cold, but different animals live at each one. For example, penguins do not live in the Arctic, only the Antarctic. Polar bears live only in the Arctic.

| amaze |
| arctic |
| court |
| elect |
| interval |
| league |
| limit |
| milestone |
| recreation |
| tackle |

interval

noun A space between two things.

noun A period of time between events.

Context Clues

These sentences give clues to the meaning of **intervals.**

*The desks were placed at two-foot **intervals,** or two feet apart.*

*The runners began the race at five-minute **intervals:** the first group started at 10:00 a.m., the next group started at 10:05 a.m., and so on.*

Discussion & Writing Prompt

A farmer plants her seeds eighteen inches apart. What is the **interval** between seeds, and how do you know?

2 min.

1. Turn and talk to your partner or group.

Use this space to take notes or draw your ideas.

3 min.

2. Write 1–3 sentences.

Be ready to share what you have written.

Study the words. Then do the exercises that follow.

chasm

n. A deep crack or opening in the earth.

When we came to the **chasm,** we saw that the only way across was an old rope bridge.

continent

n. One of the seven great land areas of the world. These are Africa, Antarctica, Asia, Australia, North America, South America, and Europe.

Because Antarctica is very cold, it is the **continent** with the fewest people.

credit

n. 1. Honor or praise; a way of expressing thanks.

After the kitten was rescued, everyone gave the **credit** to Marcia, who had quickly climbed the tree to get it.

2. A way of buying things and paying for them later.

The Simpsons bought their car on **credit** and will make car payments every month for several years.

Tell your partner about someone you give credit to because he or she helped you.

enable

v. To make possible; to give the means to bring about.

Living for a year in Greece **enabled** everyone in my family to learn to speak some Greek.

Tell your partner something that being in school has enabled you to do.

foul

adj. 1. Having an unpleasant taste or smell.

A **foul** smell of chemicals came from the jewelry polishing factory.

2. Stormy, with strong winds and heavy rain.

We biked as fast as we could to reach home before the **foul** weather hit.

n. In sports, a move or play that is against the rules.

When Steffi hit the ball outside the line, the umpire called a **foul.**

 Discuss with your partner a food you think is foul.

gust

n. A sudden increase in the strength of the wind.

As the hurricane got closer, **gusts** of wind shook the house.

ordeal

n. An unpleasant, painful, or difficult experience or test.

Lena's visit to the dentist was *not* the **ordeal** she had feared it would be.

 Tell your partner about an ordeal a friend has gone through.

plateau

n. A broad, flat area of high ground.

After a thousand-foot climb, the explorers reached the **plateau.**

rig

v. 1. To make or do something by using whatever is nearby.

Sawyer and I wanted a shady place to sit in the backyard, so we **rigged** up a tent using two broom handles and an old blanket.

2. To set up sails on a boat.

Mom **rigged** the sails while we loaded the picnic basket, towels, and life jackets on the boat.

n. A machine or construction that is used for a special purpose.

Oil **rigs** pump oil from 1,000 feet deep.

schedule

n. 1. A plan that gives expected times for different things to happen.

A flat tire put Krishna a half hour behind **schedule** on her bike trip across Michigan.

2. A list of times when trains, buses, and airplanes arrive and leave.

This **schedule** says that the last bus for Los Angeles leaves at midnight.

 Discuss with your partner the best part of your school schedule.

6A

Using Words in Context

Read the sentences. If the word in bold is used correctly, write C on the line. If the word is used incorrectly, write I on the line.

❶ (a) It was hard climbing down the steep side of the **chasm.** _____

(b) There are deep **chasms** in the ocean floor. _____

(c) Close the door to keep the **chasm** from getting out. _____

(d) The **chasm** was a hundred feet deep and over a mile long. _____

2 (a) The **gust** was so sour that I almost couldn't swallow it. _____

(b) A sudden **gust** of wind almost knocked me over. _____

(c) **Gusts** of sixty miles an hour were recorded yesterday. _____

(d) The **gusts** turned people's umbrellas inside out. _____

3 (a) A **foul** smell greeted me when I lifted the lid. _____

(b) Tripping another player on purpose is a **foul.** _____

(c) **Foul** weather made the vessel return to land. _____

(d) Ducks and turkeys were some of the **fouls** that we ate. _____

4 (a) Just getting on the school bus was an **ordeal** after Laneah hurt her foot. _____

(b) Soldiers were expected to accept their **ordeal** without fear. _____

(c) The sailors told us of their six-day **ordeal** before they were rescued. _____

(d) The player committed an **ordeal** and was sent off the field. _____

5 (a) With a hurricane approaching, the ship was **rigged** for speed. _____

(b) We **rigged** up a bed on the floor with some cushions. _____

(c) The **rig** was over fifty feet high and weighed a hundred tons. _____

(d) He was caught red-handed and can't **rig** his way out of it. _____

6 (a) Hard work **enabled** me to get better grades. _____

(b) I was **enabled** to walk after I broke my leg. _____

(c) Gravity is what **enables** us to stay on the ground. _____

(d) New drugs coming out will **enable** us to cure many diseases. _____

7 (a) The work **schedule** gives the crew every Monday off. _____

(b) The **schedule** says our train leaves from platform 2. _____

(c) Your watercolor **schedule** of the autumn tree is beautiful. _____

(d) Celia keeps a **schedule** of every movie she has ever seen. _____

8 (a) Pedro bought the bike on **credit,** planning to pay it off later. ____

(b) No one gave me **credit** for helping Jackee and Ted make up after their fight. ____

(c) With your ambition, you can easily **credit** your way to a top job. ____

(d) I **credited** the money in a tin box, which I hid. ____

6B Making Connections

Circle the letter next to the correct answer.

1 Which word goes with *Africa?*

(a) tower   (b) miner   (c) chasm   (d) continent

2 Which word goes with *sports team?*

(a) gust   (b) league   (c) motor   (d) plateau

3 Which word goes with *boat sails?*

(a) foul   (b) schedule   (c) rig   (d) span

4 Which word goes with *unpleasant?*

(a) moist   (b) suitable   (c) average   (d) foul

5 Which word goes with a *helping hand?*

(a) span   (b) enable   (c) amaze   (d) elect

6 Which word goes with *windy?*

(a) sculpture   (b) chasm   (c) plateau   (d) gust

7 Which word goes with *painful?*

(a) schedule   (b) credit   (c) ordeal   (d) process

8 Which word goes with *plan?*

(a) average   (b) rig   (c) plateau   (d) schedule

chasm
continent
credit
enable
foul
gust
ordeal
plateau
rig
schedule

6C Using Context Clues

Circle the letter next to the word that correctly completes the sentence.

1 A fifty-foot rope bridge spanned the _____.

   (a) continent   (b) plateau   (c) chasm   (d) border

2 Europeans first discovered the _____ of Australia in the 1600s.

   (a) schedule   (b) plateau   (c) league   (d) continent

3 Miss Marple believed in giving _____ where it was due.

   (a) credit   (b) process   (c) limit   (d) recreation

4 From the _____ we could look down on the valley below.

   (a) credit   (b) plateau   (c) schedule   (d) gust

5 The skipper is teaching the crew how to _____ a sailboat.

   (a) rig   (b) schedule   (c) foul   (d) limit

6 In 1920, women were _____ to vote for the first time.

   (a) scheduled   (b) rigged   (c) enabled   (d) shared

7 Check the _____ to see if there are any changes.

   (a) schedule   (b) credit   (c) rig   (d) interval

Completing Sentences

Circle each answer choice that correctly completes the sentence. Each question has three correct answers.

1 The **chasms**

(a) were caused by an ancient earthquake.

(b) are being gradually filled in.

(c) make it dangerous to travel in the area on foot.

(d) of wind blew the tent over while we were camping.

2 The **continents**

(a) of Africa and South America were once joined.

(b) and the oceans make up the planet Earth.

(c) are seven in number and do not include the Arctic.

(d) are completely covered in water.

3 **Credit**

(a) Herman for telling the truth about what happened.

(b) can be misused if you are careless with money.

(c) hides unseen just waiting to attack.

(d) offers a way to pay for things over time.

4 The **foul**

(a) was large enough to make a meal for six.

(b) got the player sent off the field.

(c) weather kept the boats close to shore.

(d) smell came from rotting food.

5 The **plateau**

(a) was cotton and had an attractive silk border.

(b) is bordered by steep cliffs on all sides.

(c) is two hundred feet above the sea.

(d) could only be reached by helicopter.

chasm
continent
credit
enable
foul
gust
ordeal
plateau
rig
schedule

Doing It the Hard Way

Antarctica is the coldest place on Earth. It is cold even during the summer months. The temperature there hardly ever gets above 30 degrees below zero. So who would want to cross this frozen land on skis? Two women from different countries wanted to try it. Let's discover what made them do it and learn what it takes to make such a journey.

· · · · · · · · · · · · · ·

For many years, both Ann Bancroft and Liv Arnesen had dreamed of crossing Antarctica. That is a distance of 2,400 miles. Ann Bancroft is a teacher from Minnesota. She says that her love of adventure began when she was ten. She gives **credit** to her mother for planting the seed. "My mom found adventure books for me to read which had females actively involved in the story."

Liv Arnesen is a teacher from Norway. She also has a great love of adventure. She, like Ann, climbed and skied in different countries. It was only a matter of time before these two women met. Once they had, they began making plans to carry out their dream of crossing Antarctica.

They decided to fly from South Africa on November 1, 2000, to Queen Maud Land on the edge of Antarctica. From there, they would cross the **continent** on skis, pulling sleds with their supplies. They both had sails to use to pull themselves along. Antarctica is very windy. Ann and Liv counted on using the wind to help them. They hoped to reach the Ross Ice Shelf on the other side of Antarctica in February. There, a ship would meet them. The ship would carry them home.

Foul weather kept them from flying to Queen Maud Land until November 13. Then Ann and Liv wasted no time strapping on their skis. They set off for the South Pole, pulling their sleds. The pole was 1,500 miles away. The first part of the trip was on bare ice and over stretches of deep snow. They had to watch out for **chasms** in the ice. The chasms could swallow them without warning. They were able to average no more than one mile an hour.

Ann and Liv climbed to over 10,000 feet above sea level. At that point they had reached the **plateau** that surrounds the South Pole. Traveling then became easier. They were able to **rig** their sails. The wind in their sails pulled them along on smooth ice at twenty-five miles an hour. Once a **gust** of wind lifted Ann clear off the ice. She found herself sailing through the air for a short time!

Each night they set up their tent. Then it was time for their evening meal. For breakfast they often had oatmeal and dried fruit. They also ate fatty foods to give them energy. Ann and Liv had telephones of the latest design; this allowed them to stay in touch with the outside world. They gave daily reports on their website. The phones **enabled** millions of school children from all over the world to follow their adventures.

When Ann and Liv reached the South Pole, they took hot showers and changed to fresh clothes. Before continuing their journey, they picked up food and supplies. The women knew they were running behind **schedule.** There were too many days without wind. If they could not use their sails, they would not reach the ship on time. On February 12, they arrived at the Ross Ice Shelf. They had crossed Antarctica. The ship, however, was still 500 miles farther on. It had to leave by February 22. After that it would be trapped by ice in the Antarctic winter.

On February 14, Ann and Liv had hundreds of miles to go. There was still very little wind. The women made a difficult decision. They asked to be picked up by an airplane with skis. The plane was standing by to help them. It carried them to the ship. They felt sadness at not completing the entire journey. But mixed with that was relief that their **ordeal** was over. Ann and Liv have spent the years since their great adventure leading parties to many parts of the world.

| chasm |
| continent |
| credit |
| enable |
| foul |
| gust |
| ordeal |
| plateau |
| rig |
| schedule |

Answer each of the following questions with a sentence. If a question does not contain a vocabulary word from the lesson's word list, use one in your answer. Use each word only once.

❶ From which **continent** did Ann and Liv leave when they flew to Queen Maud Land?

_____

_____

❷ How much time did Liv and Ann allow for their crossing?

_____

_____

❸ What two qualities would you **credit** Liv and Ann for having?

_____

_____

❹ When could it be difficult to **rig** the sails?

_____

_____

❺ Why was travel easier when they reached the area around the South Pole?

_____

_____

❻ Why did Ann and Liv go so slowly during the first part of the trip?

_____

_____

❼ What did a **gust** do while Ann was being pulled by a sail?

_____

_____

8 Why was the wind important for Ann and Liv?

_____

_____

9 Name two things that made the trip an **ordeal** for Liv and Ann.

_____

_____

10 How might Ann and Liv's sleeping bags smell after being slept in for three months?

_____

_____

Fun FACT

- Do you know the difference between **foul** and _fowl?_ These two words are homophones. They sound the same but have different spellings and meanings. A _fowl_ is a bird such as a chicken, turkey, or duck. So, a bad-tasting chicken would be a **foul** fowl!

| chasm |
| continent |
| credit |
| enable |
| foul |
| gust |
| ordeal |
| plateau |
| rig |
| schedule |

Vocabulary Extension

credit

noun A way to show something that someone has done well.

noun A way to buy something now but pay for it later.

Academic Context

In school, you get **credit** for completing your schoolwork correctly and on time.

Context Clues

These sentences give clues to the meaning of **credit**.

*My dad gave me **credit** for not spending the afternoon with my friends instead of with my grandma, even though I had wanted to.*

*My dad told me I could buy a dress on **credit** and pay for it later.*

Discussion & Writing Prompt

Tell about a time when someone gave you **credit** for something you did well.

2 min.	3 min.
1. Turn and talk to your partner or group.	**2.** Write 1–3 sentences.
Use this space to take notes or draw your ideas.	Be ready to share what you have written.

Lessons 5 & 6

Review

Hidden Message Write the word that is missing from each sentence in the boxes next to it. All the words are from Lessons 5 and 6. The shaded boxes will answer the following riddle:

I have been around for many years. I have many little holes, but I can be filled with water, and none of it will leak out. What am I?

1. The magician put on a show that continued to _____ us days later.

2. There was a summer-long _____ between our last day of school in one year and the first day in the next.

3. I can't begin to tell you what a(n) _____ it was to speak in front of the whole school.

4. The candidate's signs read "Vote for Me" and "_____ Me!"

5. Rafael had no money, so he bought his suit on _____.

6. Our skiing trip would have been nicer without the _____ cold.

7. Imelda and Lin are on the tennis _____ waiting for you.

8. The ferryboat arrived right on _____ at 5 o'clock.

9. It was my idea to _____ up a swing made from an old car tire.

10. After eating all the grapes, I was full. I had reached my _____.

11. Australia is the world's smallest _____.

12. A sudden _____ of wind blew the newspapers away.

13. Before Elyse went fishing, she cleaned her _____ box and made it neater.

14. From the wide, flat _____ we could see for miles.

15. Kit's ability with languages will _____ her to get a job almost anywhere in the world.

Study the words. Then do the exercises that follow.

act

n. 1. Something that is done.

Giving clothes and food to the family who lost everything in the house fire was a generous **act.**

2. A show that is put on.

One **act** in the spring festival will be a Guatemalan folk dance.

3. One of the main parts of a play.

During the interval between **acts** one and two, we can walk outside for some fresh air.

v. 1. To do something.

Ellie **acted** at once when I asked her to help me move the sofa.

2. To play a part in a play, a movie, or on television.

In *The Wizard of Oz*, Bert Lahr **acted** the part of the cowardly lion.

Show your partner what it looks like when your hands are in the act of fluttering.

additional

adj. Added or extra.

Andres brought an **additional** bottle of water to the tennis court because the day was quite warm.

advice

n. Ideas or suggestions offered to help someone with a problem or situation.

Gary asked Selena for **advice** about training his frisky dog Peanuts.

Give your partner some advice about how to be a good friend.

crumple

v. To crush together; to bend or press into creases or wrinkles.

Sue's shirt was **crumpled** after she stuffed it into the bottom of her bag and forgot about it.

fan

n. 1. Something that causes air to move in order to cool whatever it blows on. Some are made of folded stiff material and can be spread open for use; others are machines with blades that run on electricity.

On hot summer days, the ceiling **fan** keeps the living room very comfortable.

2. Someone who closely follows a group, team, or person.

The **fans** cheered loudly when their soccer team ran onto the field.

v. 1. To move air with an open fan or something similar.

Gracie **fanned** herself with a folded newspaper.

2. (Often used with *out*.) To spread in the shape of an opened fan.

The students **fanned** out over the park, picking up any paper trash or empty bottles they found.

 Tell your partner a sports team you are a fan of.

memorize

v. To fix in one's memory exactly; to learn by heart.

It amazes me how quickly Jerrard can **memorize** the words of a song he has heard.

mystify

v. To confuse or puzzle someone.

How Colleen was able to find the right card **mystified** all of us.

 Discuss something that mystifies you with your partner.

pause

v. To stop for a short time before going on.

Ms. Bonnaire **paused** to see if we had questions and then finished giving us the directions for the game.

n. A short break or rest from what has been going on.

After a short **pause** to catch her breath, Alexis set off for the top of the hill.

Start talking about your favorite food. In the middle of a sentence, pause for ten seconds to look at your partner. Then finish your sentence.

transparent

adj. Allowing light to pass through freely so that one can see clearly.

Several kinds of fish swam past us in the **transparent** waters of the lake.

vanish

v. To go out of sight; to disappear.

As the ship headed out into the channel, the land **vanished** under a layer of early morning fog.

7A Words and Their Meanings

Look at the group of words next to the number. Then circle the letter next to the word that has the same meaning.

1 to learn by heart

(a) memorize   (b) act   (c) vanish   (d) pause

2 to pass out of sight

(a) crumple   (b) fan   (c) mystify   (d) vanish

3 to crush into a small space

   (a) act   (b) pause   (c) crumple   (d) mystify

4 a part of a play

   (a) advice   (b) act   (c) pause   (d) fan

Look at the word next to the number. Then circle the letter next to the group of words that has the same meaning.

5 advice

   (a) weak excuses   (b) empty spaces
   (c) helpful suggestions   (d) broken promises

6 pause

   (a) to move up and down   (b) to stop before continuing
   (c) to tread lightly   (d) to balance two different things

7 fan

   (a) to turn away from   (b) to sink lower
   (c) to offer support   (d) to cool by moving air

8 mystify

   (a) to confuse or puzzle   (b) to grasp or understand
   (c) to thicken or harden   (d) to absorb or soak up

act
additional
advice
crumple
fan
memorize
mystify
pause
transparent
vanish

Just the Right Word

Replace each phrase in bold with a single word (or form of the word) from the word list.

1 Elizabeth Taylor was twelve years old when she **played a part** in the movie *National Velvet*.

2 The glass is **able to let light pass through freely.**

3 When a reporter asked how the crocodile escaped from its pen, the zookeeper said she was **unable to understand how it had happened.**

4 The bird-watchers **moved away from each other and spread** out when they reached the woods.

5 The black panther **could no longer be seen when it went** into the night.

6 When we were buying tickets for the Ice Capades, we learned that there is an **extra and therefore higher than usual** charge for front-row seats.

7 The speaker **took a short break** for questions before she showed the video.

8 We found the letter **crushed into a ball** and thrown behind the door.

7C

Applying Meanings
Circle the letter next to the correct answer.

1 Which of the following is a piece of **advice?**
- (a) "Are you lost?"
- (b) "Take your time."
- (c) "Go to your room at once!"
- (d) "My coat is blue."

2 Why might you **crumple** a shirt?
- (a) to hang it up in a closet
- (b) to keep it clean
- (c) to make it fit in a small space
- (d) to see if it fits you

3 Which of the following should you **memorize?**
- (a) your phone number
- (b) the dictionary
- (c) the weather report
- (d) the telephone book

4 Where are you likely to see a **fan** of the painter Picasso?
- (a) in a train station
- (b) on a fishing boat
- (c) at an art museum
- (d) at a ball game

5 Which of the following can be **transparent?**
- (a) gold
- (b) water
- (c) mud
- (d) blood

6 During which of the following can there be a **pause?**
- (a) a sneeze
- (b) a wink
- (c) a song
- (d) a hiccup

7 When is it important to **act** quickly?
- (a) when you choose a book to read
- (b) when you pick a baby's name
- (c) when you decide to take a nap
- (d) when you smell something burning

act
additional
advice
crumple
fan
memorize
mystify
pause
transparent
vanish

Word Study: Latin Roots

Fill in the blank with the correct word. The number at the end of the sentence gives the lesson the word is from.

You know that a prefix is added to the beginning of a word and a suffix is added to the end. Both can change its meaning. The part of a word between the prefix and the suffix is called the base word. Let's look at the word *unsuitable*. *Un-* is a prefix, and *–able* is a suffix. *Suit* is the base word.

Sometimes the base word is a root. A lot of roots come from Latin, the language the ancient Romans spoke. If you know the meaning of the root, you can more easily figure out the meaning of the word.

1 The Latin *vanus* means "empty." If everything in a room were to _____, the room would look empty. (7)

2 The Latin *credere* means "to believe." If you find it hard to _____ someone's story, you really don't believe it. (6)

3 The Latin *plattus* means "flat." A _____ is an area of land that is high above sea level and fairly flat. (6)

4 The Latin *legere* means "to choose." When we _____ a president, we have chosen that person to move into the Oval Office of the White House. (5)

5 The Latin *coccum* means "a berry." The _____ of an insect is hard and round like a berry. (4)

6 The prefix *trans-* means "through" and is joined to the root formed from the Latin word *parere*, which means "to show." If something is _____, an object on the other side would show through it. (7)

Abracadabra!

Have you ever watched someone doing magic tricks? Have you wished that you could do some too? Would you like to discover how they are done? The secret is simple and can be told in just three words: Practice. Practice. Practice.

• • • • • • • • • • • • • •

Before you try the magic tricks that follow, here is some **advice.** Never miss a chance to make those watching you laugh. When people are laughing, they are less likely to follow what your hands are doing. Now here are three tricks that anyone can do—with a little practice, of course.

First, let's learn how to make a coin disappear by magic. You need two sheets of white paper and a **transparent** drinking glass. You'll also need a handkerchief and a coin. Take one of the sheets of paper and place the glass, upside down, over it. Draw a circle around the rim. Cut around the line you have drawn. Then glue the paper circle to the rim of the glass. Now you are ready. Place the coin on the other sheet of white paper with the glass next to it. No one sees the paper circle you have glued to the rim. All they see is an empty glass resting on the piece of paper. Keep talking as you do each step. That's so no one thinks to ask to see the glass. Take the handkerchief and place it over the glass. Cover the glass completely. Pick up the glass and place it over the coin. Say a magic word. Then remove the handkerchief. The coin has **vanished.** Only you know that it is hidden under the paper glued to the glass.

Now here is a card trick sure to **mystify** those who watch you do it. Take a deck of cards and remove the four jacks. **Fan** them out and hold them up. Everyone sees you holding up four jacks. Actually, you are holding up eight cards, not four. You have hidden four **additional** cards behind the jack that is closest to you as you hold them up. They can be any cards. Keeping the four extra cards hidden is what takes practice. Now bring the eight cards together.

act
additional
advice
crumple
fan
memorize
mystify
pause
transparent
vanish

Place them face down on top of the deck. Without letting anyone see their faces, pick up the top four cards. Place these cards anywhere in the middle of the deck. Say some magic words. Then, one by one, lift the top four cards. Each one is a jack that in some strange way has made its way from the middle of the deck to the top.

The third and last trick takes practice and a good memory. Begin by asking someone on your left to **crumple** up a dollar bill and throw it to you. Catch the bill. Then, without looking at it, throw what seems to be this bill to a person on your right. You ask them to unfold it. Have them check as you call out the number printed on the dollar bill. When you do this correctly, people are amazed.

Yet the trick is quite simple. You have your own dollar bill, and you have **memorized** the number printed on it. Before you begin the trick, you keep this crushed dollar bill hidden in your hand. You catch the dollar bill thrown to you. But it is your own dollar bill, which was hidden in your hand, that you throw for someone to catch. Be sure to practice the catching and throwing of the dollar bill before you try it in front of other people. You end your trick by saying to the person who threw you the dollar bill, "Thank you for helping me." Then you **pause** and add one more thing. "The gentleman (or lady) over there owes you a dollar." This usually gets a laugh.

Take some time to practice these and other magic tricks. You will be amazing your friends and family with your own magic **act** in no time. Good luck and remember: Abracadabra!

Answer each of the following questions with a sentence. If a question does not contain a vocabulary word from the lesson's word list, use one in your answer. Use each word only once.

. . . .

1 Why should you **pause** after saying, "Thank you for helping me"?

_____

_____

2 What do you have to be especially careful about when doing the card trick?

_____

_____

3 Name two helpful suggestions about doing magic tricks that you learned from the story.

_____

_____

4 Why must the glass with the paper glued to it be **transparent?**

_____

_____

5 Can a magician make any object **vanish** with the glass trick? Explain your answer.

_____

_____

6 Why do you want to keep the people from asking questions as they watch you?

_____

_____

7 Why do you think magicians are not likely to tell their **fans** how they do their magic tricks?

_____

_____

8 What is one skill you must have to do the trick with the dollar bill?

_____

_____

act
additional
advice
crumple
fan
memorize
mystify
pause
transparent
vanish

9 What do you think would be the hardest part of the trick with the **crumpled** dollar bill?

_____

_____

10 In your opinion, what is the best thing about watching a magic **act?**

_____

_____

Fun FACT

· ·

- **Advice** is a noun. It is something that is given, such as help or suggestions. The verb form is advise. To *advise* is to offer help or suggestions.

transparent

adjective Able to be seen through.

Word Parts

The prefix *trans-* means "through" or "across."

Discussion & Writing Prompt

Besides **transparent,** other words with the prefix *trans-* are *transmit* and *transfer.* What are some other words with the prefix *trans-?*

2 min.

1. Turn and talk to your partner or group.

Use this space to take notes or draw your ideas.

3 min.

2. Write 1–3 sentences.

Be ready to share what you have written.

Study the words. Then do the exercises that follow.

contain

v. To hold; to have within itself.

A drop of pond water **contains** thousands of tiny living creatures.

container *n.* A jar, box, or other object used for holding something.

Martina and Sam loved visiting the bead shop where small square **containers** held beads of many different colors, sizes, and shapes.

 Tell your partner something your classroom contains.

digest

v. To change food that has been eaten into simpler forms that the body can use.

Because Janine cannot **digest** milk, her parents give her soy drinks.

finicky

adj. Hard to please; fussy.

Adriana knew her parents would think she was being **finicky,** but she was just not hungry.

habit

n. 1. Something that a person does so often that it is done without thinking.

Katie's **habit** of saying "you know" after every sentence is annoying.

2. A special kind of clothing worn by certain groups.

A very important part of a riding **habit** is the hard helmet to protect the head in case of a fall.

 Tell your partner about a bad habit you want to stop.

hinge

n. A joint on a lid or door that allows it to swing open or shut.

Roger oiled the steel **hinges** on our front gate from time to time so they would not rust.

 Put your hands together to pretend they are a door. Use your hands to show your partner where a hinge is on a door.

marsh

n. A low-lying area, often covered with tall grasses, where the ground is soft and wet.

The **marshes** near Long Island Sound provide a home for many snails, crabs, and minnows.

marshy *adj.* Soft and moist underfoot.

Reeds and cattails grow in the **marshy** area near the lake.

nursery

n. 1. A room or other place set aside for the use of babies and small children.

On our visit to the hospital, we stopped by the **nursery** to take a look at our new cousin, who was sleeping peacefully.

2. A place where plants are grown for sale.

On Saturday, Uncle Karl and Aunt Ruby went to the **nursery** to choose two locust trees to plant in front of their house.

rely

v. To count on; to look to for support.

When they asked Diane if they could **rely** on her to deliver the secret message to the right person, she said, "Of course!"

reliable *adj.* Trustworthy; not likely to fail.

Until he could repair the brakes, Dad said our car was not **reliable** enough for a long trip.

 Tell your partner why you think you are a reliable person.

spine

n. 1. The backbone.

The **spine** protects the nerves that run from the brain to every part of the body.

2. A thin, sharp, stiff part that sticks out on certain plants and animals.

The one-inch-long **spines** on a prickly pear cactus have been used to make toothpicks and needles.

thrive

v. To do well; to grow strong and healthy.

Lavender plants **thrive** in sunny spots without too much water.

 Discuss with your partner an animal that would thrive in your area.

Using Words in Context

Read the sentences. If the word in bold is used correctly, write C on the line. If the word is used incorrectly, write I on the line.

1 (a) **Marshes** are covered with tall grasses. _____

(b) The **marsh** formed a deep crack in the pie's crust. _____

(c) Tikei was in a **marshy** mood, so we kept out of her way. _____

(d) Your feet may sink in **marshy** ground. _____

2 (a) **Nurseries** grow well in the soil between the rivers. _____

(b) The mother visited the **nursery** where her new baby was sleeping. _____

(c) The local **nursery** is having a sale on tomato plants. _____

(d) The woolen **nursery** hung loosely around Jan's shoulders. _____

3 (a) Water becomes more **reliable** as it gets colder. _____

(b) You can't trust Yeye, because she is very **reliable**. _____

(c) Our car is ten years old but is still very **reliable**. _____

(d) She promised me I could **rely** on her help if I needed it. _____

4 (a) The space station **contains** everything we need to stay alive. _____

(b) This sentence **contains** just six words. _____

(c) The prince was the king's loyal **container**. _____

(d) I used an old coffee can as a **container** for my pen collection. _____

contain
digest
finicky
habit
hinge
marsh
nursery
rely
spine
thrive

5 (a) The human **spine** is made up of twenty-six bones. _____

(b) The **spines** on the plant keep animals from eating the plant. _____

(c) Porcupines have very sharp **spines**. _____

(d) The Earth spins on its **spine** every twenty-four hours. _____

6 (a) Heat up the **habit** if you are cold. _____

(b) Foxes make their **habits** in holes in the ground. _____

(c) Rose's **habit** of rolling her eyes is very annoying. _____

(d) Her riding **habit** was complete, from hat to boots. _____

7 (a) The baby lion is really **thriving** since it was rescued. ____

(b) **Thrive** is a dish that can be eaten hot or cold. ____

(c) The country **thrived** when she was president. ____

(d) José **thrived** to escape the small village where he grew up. ____

8 (a) The little boy got more and more **finicky** and then just started crying. ____

(b) I can be quite **finicky** when it comes to choosing a dentist. ____

(c) His hands were all **finicky** with peanut butter. ____

(d) Shania is very **finicky** and won't eat anything that comes out of a can. ____

8B Making Connections
Circle the letter next to the correct answer.

1 Which word goes with *stomach?*

(a) spine   b) digest   (c) nursery   (d) thrive

2 Which word goes with *clothing?*

(a) transparent   (b) hinge   (c) container   (d) habit

3 Which word goes with *door?*

(a) spine   (b) milestone   (c) rig   (d) hinge

4 Which word goes with *plants?*

(a) habit   (b) chasm   (c) nursery   (d) credit

5 Which word goes with *moist?*

(a) plateau   (b) hinge   (c) spine   (d) marsh

6 Which word goes with *trusted?*

(a) reliable   (b) amazing   (c) finicky   (d) moist

7 Which word goes with *holder?*

(a) spine   (b) container   (c) hinge   (d) border

8 Which word goes with *cactus?*

(a) arctic   (b) spine   (c) marsh   (d) habit

8C Using Context Clues

Circle the letter next to the word that correctly completes the sentence.

1 Some people find that they cannot _____ milk products.

(a) vanish   (b) thrive   (c) contain   (d) digest

2 When it comes to buying new clothes, some people can be quite _____.

(a) additional   (b) finicky   (c) reliable   (d) average

3 A rusty _____ will not work correctly.

(a) nursery   (b) hinge   (c) habit   (d) pause

4 Telling lies is a bad _____.

(a) container   (b) marsh   (c) habit   (d) hinge

5 The large jug _____ two cups of milk.

(a) enables   (b) contains   (c) digests   (d) spans

6 Walk carefully because the ground is _____.

(a) finicky   (b) reliable   (c) gusty   (d) marshy

7 The new owners of Oak Farm have opened a _____.

(a) continent   (b) nursery   (c) marsh   (d) plateau

contain
digest
finicky
habit
hinge
marsh
nursery
rely
spine
thrive

8D Completing Sentences

Circle each answer choice that correctly completes the sentence. Each question has three correct answers.

1 Pet rabbits **thrive**

(a) hard to please their parents.

(b) when put on this special diet.

(c) if they are kept warm and dry.

(d) when they are loved and protected.

2 A **reliable**

(a) map is one that is not out of date.

(b) weather forecast has a good chance of being true.

(c) horse will always throw off its rider.

(d) friend is one you can count on.

3 The **hinges**

(a) need to be screwed in place tightly.

(b) tell you when to pause the music for a few seconds.

(c) were made of solid gold.

(d) work better if they aren't rusty.

4 Roberto is **finicky**

(a) and easily pleased.

(b) about whom he invites to his home.

(c) when it comes to what he eats.

(d) about everything except his hair.

5 Meat is **digested**

(a) more easily if it is cooked.

(b) in a long process that begins in the mouth.

(c) best if it is properly chewed.

(d) in the oven until it is tender.

Danger: Hungry Plants

Everyone knows that animals eat plants. There is nothing unusual about that. But have you heard about plants that eat animals? Let's discover where some of them live. Let's learn how they get their food.

· · · · · · · · · · · · · ·

Growing in the wild only along the coast of North and South Carolina is a plant with unusual eating **habits.** It is called the Venus flytrap. It grows well in the sunny weather that the Carolinas enjoy most of the year. The best places to see it are in **marshy** areas where the soil is poor. Poor soil does not matter to the Venus flytrap. It is different from most plants. The Venus flytrap does not **rely** on its roots to supply the food it needs.

The Venus flytrap grows to a height of about twelve inches and has little white flowers. Each of its leaves has a **hinge** running down the middle with a row of tiny **spines** along each side. When an insect lands on one of them, the leaf snaps shut, trapping the creature inside like a prisoner behind bars.

The center of each leaf is a rich red color. To a fly this looks like raw meat. That is exactly what flies like to feed on. The plant also has a sweet smell. This attracts other insects. The Venus flytrap is not **finicky.** It eats whatever it can catch. That includes different kinds of insects and ants. It even eats small frogs or lizards. Once attracted by the smell, an insect coming closer has no idea of the danger it is in. The insect sees what looks like fresh meat. It lands. Then the leaf closes on the creature. The insect can't break free. The more it struggles, the tighter it is held. The plant then starts to **digest** its meal. It does this in much the same way your stomach breaks down the food you eat. In a week to ten days, the plant has absorbed everything it needs. The leaf then opens and gets rid of what is left.

contain
digest
finicky
habit
hinge
marsh
nursery
rely
spine
thrive

You do not have to go to North or South Carolina to see these interesting plants. You can grow them yourself at home. A **nursery** will sell you young plants. The Venus flytrap plant will **thrive** in a goldfish bowl or large glass jar. Place a few inches of wet moss mixed with sand in the bottom of the bowl. Cover the roots of the plant with it. Keep the temperature around seventy-five degrees during the summer months. In winter, move the plant to a cooler spot, around forty degrees.

Make sure the sand mixture stays moist during the growing season. Water it a little each day instead of letting it get dry and then soaking it. Rainwater is better than water from the tap. To feed the Venus flytrap, drop a couple of live ants or small insects into the **container** from time to time. Keep it covered so that the insects cannot escape. Place it in a spot where it gets plenty of light. Then watch what happens.

Answer each of the following questions with a sentence. If a question does not contain a vocabulary word from the lesson's word list, use one in your answer. Use each word only once.

1 Is the Venus flytrap **finicky** about where it grows in the wild? Explain.

_____

_____

2 Why might the Venus flytrap not **thrive** in a cold, cloudy climate?

_____

_____

3 Why is the Venus flytrap able to live in poor **marshy** soil?

_____

_____

4 Where else besides the Carolinas can you find Venus flytrap plants?

_____

_____

5 Which part of the plant does the Venus flytrap depend on for its food?

_____

_____

6 What do a door and a Venus flytrap leaf have in common?

_____

_____

7 What are the **spines** of a Venus flytrap for?

_____

_____

8 In what way are humans and Venus flytrap plants alike?

_____

_____

9 What makes a suitable **container** for a Venus flytrap?

_____

_____

10 What should you do each day to care for your Venus flytrap?

_____

_____

contain
digest
finicky
habit
hinge
marsh
nursery
rely
spine
thrive

Fun FACT

• Know your textbook! The part of a book where the pages are gathered, then glued or sewn together, made the first bookmakers think of the human backbone, or **spine**. That part of a book is called the spine still today. It supports the book, just as our spines support our bodies.

rely

verb To depend on someone for support.

Word Family

reliable (adjective)
reliance (noun)
unreliable (adjective)

Discussion & Writing Prompt

Write about a time when you had to **rely** on someone to help you.

2 min.	3 min.
1. Turn and talk to your partner or group.	2. Write 1–3 sentences.
Use this space to take notes or draw your ideas.	Be ready to share what you have written.

Lessons 7 & 8

Review

Crossword Puzzle Solve the puzzle by writing the missing word in each sentence in the boxes with the matching numbers. All the words are from Lessons 7 and 8.

ACROSS

2. We could see inside the _____ plastic bag.

4. Eat crackers; they're easy to _____.

5. Everyone clapped after the play's first _____ .

8. When our cat is ill, we ask our vet for _____.

10. The lid of the old chest had a squeaky _____.

12. This small _____ turns on when the machine becomes too hot.

13. The marigolds will _____ in a sunny area.

14. The daily tide keeps a saltwater _____ alive.

16. The gift we bought cost twenty dollars. Tax was a(n) _____ dollar.

17. When reading aloud, you should _____ at the end of a sentence.

18. That magic trick will not _____ anyone over six years old.

19. Can I _____ on you to keep a secret?

DOWN

1. These delicious oatmeal cookies seem to _____ as soon as they come out of the oven.

3. A porcupine's sharp _____ protect it from enemies.

6. To make this juice, we need a(n) _____ that holds two quarts.

7. Will you _____ your speech or read from notes?

9. I saw him _____ the paper and toss it into the wastebasket.

11. Each spring the _____ sells young fruit trees and lilac bushes.

12. Shopping for clothes with my cousin always takes a long time because he is so _____.

15. Kate's _____ of humming all the time is very annoying.

Study the words. Then do the exercises that follow.

attitude

n. A way of thinking or feeling about certain things.

Unhappy and grouchy before lunch, Tina had quite a different **attitude** after she had eaten something.

Tell your partner your attitude about homework.

confess

v. To say or admit that one has done something wrong.

When my sister accused me of getting spots on her best sweater, I **confessed** that I had, but by accident.

defend

v. 1. To keep from being attacked; to protect.

The mother goose **defended** her young by beating her wings as she ran toward us, hissing.

2. To speak for; to argue in favor of.

My cousin **defended** me when my brother complained that I never helped with the dishes.

Talk with your partner about how you could defend a friend who was late to school.

gradual

adj. Happening slowly; taking place little by little.

The rising sea level is caused by the **gradual** melting of the ice cap in Antarctica.

Show your partner how you can open your mouth a gradual bit at a time.

hint

n. Information given to help someone answer a question; a clue.

Mr. Wang said he would not give us any **hints** until we had tried to solve the puzzle.

v. To suggest something without saying directly what one means.

Rosa had **hinted** so often about wanting a puppy for her birthday that her parents finally got her one.

individual

n. A single person, apart from others in a group.

When the teacher asked everyone in class who knew the answer to stand up, only one **individual** stood.

adj. Meant for just one.

At the kennel, the dogs were kept in **individual** cages.

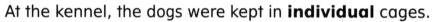

 Talk with your partner about how each individual cloud in the sky is different.

malice

n. The wish to hurt others on purpose.

Although Camilla feels no **malice** toward whoever stole her wallet, she is going to be angry if it is not returned.

malicious *adj.* Done with a wish to harm or cause pain.

Everyone agreed that spray painting words on the side of the new store was a **malicious** thing to do.

misery

    n. A feeling of great unhappiness.

    The flash flood brought **misery** to hundreds of families whose homes were now standing in four feet of water.

    miserable *adj.* 1. Very unhappy or unpleasant.

    The mosquitoes were so thick in the woods that I was **miserable** for the entire hike.

    2. Very bad; of poor quality.

    We discovered what a **miserable** job the roofer had done when we found a leak in the attic after the next rainstorm.

solution

    n. 1. The answer to a problem or puzzle.

    After filling in all but a few of the blanks in the crossword puzzle, Rico turned to the back of the newspaper for the **solution.**

    2. A mixture formed when a liquid and some other materials are mixed together.

    Brine, which is a **solution** of salt and water, keeps pickles crisp and fresh.

survey

    v. To look over; to examine.

    From a helicopter, the governor **surveyed** the damage caused by the tornado.

    n. A study designed to gather information about a subject.

    Our class made a **survey** of all students to find out which lunches were most popular.

With your partner, survey your classroom to see how many people have long hair and how many people have short hair.

9A

Words and Their Meanings

Look at the group of words next to the number. Then circle the letter next to the word that has the same meaning.

1 the wish to hurt someone
(a) attitude   (b) hint   (c) individual   (d) malice

2 taking place slowly
(a) malicious   (b) miserable   (c) gradual   (d) individual

3 a way of thinking
(a) misery   (b) solution   (c) survey   (d) attitude

4 an indirect suggestion
(a) solution   (b) hint   (c) survey   (d) misery

Look at the word next to the number. Then circle the letter next to the group of words that has the same meaning.

5 confess
(a) to cause fear or alarm   (b) to care for
(c) to join together   (d) to admit you have done wrong

attitude
confess
defend
gradual
hint
individual
malice
misery
solution
survey

6 solution
(a) the answer to a problem   (b) a frozen liquid
(c) a slow process   (d) a mystery

7 defend
(a) to bring to an end   (b) to search for
(c) to keep from harm   (d) to place limits on

8 survey
(a) to warn of danger   (b) to take a look at
(c) to give shelter to   (d) to guess at an answer

1. At their first practice, the soccer players decided which **person from all the others** on the team would keep track of the balls.

2. I told my friend Nat that I could not **speak in favor of** what he did because it was wrong.

3. The **study designed to get information on the subject** shows that over half of the students speak more than one language.

4. Tamara's **very unpleasant** day began when she overslept and then arrived late to school.

5. This **mixture made up** of sugar and water attracts many hummingbirds to our feeder.

6. Mark **suggested without saying so directly** that he would like a second piece of pie.

7. The melting of the ice on the pond was **taking place very slowly,** so it was more than a week before it was gone.

8. Although my uncle did not say his words with **the wish to cause pain,** my father still felt hurt and a little angry.

Applying Meanings
Circle the letter next to the correct answer.

1 To which of the following might a person **confess?**
(a) winning a prize
(b) memorizing a poem
(c) making a new friend
(d) hurting someone on purpose

2 How might you **defend** yourself?
(a) by speaking up
(b) by eating lunch
(c) by laughing
(d) by going to sleep

3 Where will you find **individual** places set up?
(a) on a football field
(b) on a mountain
(c) at a dining table
(d) on a basketball court

4 Which of the following is a sign of **misery?**
(a) weeping
(b) laughing
(c) smiling
(d) sneezing

5 Which of the following might be a **hint?**
(a) Don't do that again!
(b) We sell pizza by the slice.
(c) Where is my toothbrush?
(d) I am pink and can fly.

6 What information might a **survey** show?
(a) a recipe for fried rice
(b) the favorite recreation of kids age six to ten
(c) the distance to the moon
(d) the normal body temperature in humans

7 To which of the following might there be a **solution?**
(a) a joke
(b) a schedule
(c) an award
(d) a riddle

attitude
confess
defend
gradual
hint
individual
malice
misery
solution
survey

9D Word Study: Synonyms

In each group of three words, decide which two are synonyms and circle them.

Two words that have the same or almost the same meaning are called synonyms. *Big* and *large* are synonyms.

1 confess act admit

2 defend crumple protect

3 hint suggest digest

4 survey enable examine

5 memorize contain hold

6 reliable average trustworthy

7 elect choose amaze

8 disappear vanish flutter

Bully Solutions

Do kids tease each other at your school? Teasing is normal. Most of the time, it is harmless. But sometimes teasing crosses the line. Then it becomes bullying, which is a serious problem.

• • • • • • • • • • • • •

Teasing becomes bullying when it is done with **malice.** Pushing and shoving and even fights can take place. The U.S. Department of Justice conducted a **survey** in 2010. The results of this study showed that one in five kids has been bullied.

Schools have tried different **solutions** to the bullying problem. One started a "Bully-Buster Box." Students could report any bullying they saw by dropping notes into the box. They did not have to sign their names if they chose not to. This scared some bullies. They were not so quick to pick on someone if they knew they would be reported. Another school had student meetings once a week. The students sat in a circle and talked face-to-face. At these meetings, the bullies were sometimes the first to **confess.** They often felt guilty and unhappy about their actions.

In the last several years, there has been a **gradual** rise in Internet bullying. If you are like many young people, you go on the Internet. You send or receive e-mails. You might even like to talk on chat rooms or social networking sites. If you do any of those things, you should learn more about bullying online.

Online bullies have a bad **attitude,** and they can do some very bad things. They may send mean, hurtful messages to **individuals.** That can make anyone feel **miserable.** If you get a mean or scary message and feel you are being bullied, there are steps you can take to **defend** yourself. Delete all messages from the bully without reading or opening them. Over time, this may cause the bully to take the **hint** and leave you alone. If your friends are being bullied, tell them to do the same. The best thing you can do is tell a parent or teacher what is happening. This information is key to stopping

| attitude |
| confess |
| defend |
| gradual |
| hint |
| individual |
| malice |
| misery |
| solution |
| survey |

bullies. Finally, a good relationship between adults and students is the most helpful thing of all.

Answer each of the following questions with a sentence. If a question does not contain a vocabulary word from the lesson's word list, use one in your answer. Use each word only once.

● ●

1 When does teasing cross the line and become **malicious?**

_____

_____

2 Has the rise in Internet bullying happened suddenly?

_____

_____

3 What do you think it means that bullies have a bad **attitude?**

_____

_____

4 Why do you think the passage gives several ways to deal with the problem of bullying in schools?

_____

_____

5 Why might deleting a bully's e-mails without reading them be a good way to **defend** yourself?

_____

_____

6 Where did some of the information in the passage on bullying come from?

_____

_____

7 Why might getting a mean, scary message make someone feel **miserable?**

_____

_____

8 Why is it that some bullies feel the need to **confess?**

_____

_____

9 Why might a bullying e-mail message be especially upsetting to an **individual?**

_____

_____

10 What is the final helpful **hint** contained in the passage?

_____

_____

| attitude |
| confess |
| defend |
| gradual |
| hint |
| individual |
| malice |
| misery |
| solution |
| survey |

Fun FACT

• The antonym, or opposite, of **defend** is _offend_. One meaning of _defend_ is "to protect from being attacked"; one meaning of _offend_ is the exact opposite, "to attack." You may have heard forms of the words as they are used in sports. In football and basketball, for example, the team with the ball on _offense_ is trying to score against (attack) the other team. The team on _defense_, the team without the ball, is trying not to be scored upon (attacked).

individual

noun A single person who is apart from others in a group.

adjective Single; for only one.

Word Family

individuality (noun)

individualized (adjective)

individually (adverb)

Discussion & Writing Prompt

In school, sometimes you work in a group, and sometimes you work **individually.** What do you work on **individually** in school?

2 min.	3 min.
1. Turn and talk to your partner or group.	**2.** Write 1–3 sentences.
Use this space to take notes or draw your ideas.	Be ready to share what you have written.

Study the words. Then do the exercises that follow.

cable

> *n.* 1. A thick steel rope made of strands of wire twisted together.
>
> A **cable** with a large hook on the end dangled from the top of the crane.
>
> 2. A bundle of wires covered by rubber or plastic along which an electric current can pass.
>
> The electric company will run an underground **cable** from this station to Quincy to provide extra power when it is needed.

cathedral

> *n.* A large and important church.
>
> The National **Cathedral** in Washington, D.C., is the sixth largest in the world.

convey

> *v.* 1. To carry or move from one place to another.
>
> A wagon with high sides **conveyed** the cut sugarcane to the mill.
>
> 2. To make an idea or feeling known.
>
> As the curtain closed, the crowd clapped loudly to **convey** how much they had enjoyed the play.

 •

Convey to your partner your thoughts about some music you like.

device

n. Something made or invented for a particular use.

When you need a **device** for lifting heavy weights without a great deal of effort, a lever will work best.

Talk with your partner about a helpful device in your home.

freight

n. Goods carried from place to place, as by plane, boat, truck, or train.

The trains passing through this station carry **freight** from the middle of the country to the East Coast.

landmark

n. 1. A building or natural feature that is easy to see and can be used as a guide.

The Gateway Arch is a well-known **landmark** in St. Louis.

2. An important event.

The discovery that certain bacteria can cause disease was a **landmark** in the history of medicine.

Tell your partner about a famous landmark in your country.

method

n. A way of doing something.

Tara's **method** for bringing her cat inside is to shake the container with treats.

Tell your partner about your method for washing your hands.

rod

n. A thin, straight piece of wood, metal, or other material.

The shower curtain hung from a metal **rod.**

shaft

> *n.* 1. A long open tunnel that runs straight up and down.
>
> The coal miners traveled for five minutes to reach the bottom of the mine **shaft.**
>
> 2. A bar that connects with other moving parts of a machine.
>
> The drive **shaft** sends power from the car engine to the wheels.
>
> 3. The long, narrow part of an arrow or other object.
>
> Felix made sure the **shafts** of his arrows were in a straight line.

structure

> *n.* Something that is built, as a building or bridge.
>
> From the road, it was easy to see that the largest **structure** in town was the hundred-foot water tower.

· ·

Discuss with your partner a structure near your school.

Using Words in Context

Read the sentences. If the word in bold is used correctly, write C on the line. If the word is used incorrectly, write I on the line.

❶ (a) Each **device** is tested before it leaves the factory. _____

(b) The **device** hatched after ten days. _____

(c) He wrote the **device** beautifully. _____

(d) The **device** is designed to help kids clean their rooms. _____

2 (a) We rigged the sails on the forty-foot **shaft** and set off for Hawaii. _____

(b) The mining crew went down the **shaft** in a metal cage. _____

(c) The **shaft** of the arrow was placed in the bow and then aimed. _____

(d) Great **shafts** of fish were pushed toward land by the dolphins. _____

3 (a) Please **convey** the message to your mom that I hope she gets better soon. _____

(b) I could **convey** no meaning from the old letter. _____

(c) Moving belts **convey** the items to the next stage of the process. _____

(d) The Statue of Liberty in New York harbor **conveys** the idea of freedom. _____

4 (a) The **cable** is best eaten with honey and bread. _____

(b) Electric **cables** carry power to every home in the city. _____

(c) He arrived in a four-wheel **cable** pulled by two horses. _____

(d) The first **cable** to send messages through electricity was laid in 1858. _____

5 (a) Electing the first woman president was a **landmark** event. _____

(b) The Statue of Liberty is a familiar New York **landmark.** _____

(c) A **landmark** was sealed inside the bag to be eaten later. _____

(d) I told my teacher I'd **landmark** my homework to make it better. _____

6 (a) Oil is moved by **freight** train or by pipes. _____

(b) Boats are sometimes used to carry **freight.** _____

(c) I have never felt so much **freight** as when Keith jumped out and scared me. _____

(d) Sending **freight** to the space station is very expensive. _____

7 (a) Slugger told me to find my own **method** for swinging the bat. ____

(b) Rubbing two sticks together is one **method** of starting a fire. ____

(c) What **method** do you use for watering your plants? ____

(d) The **method** we followed was a twisting path that led to the lighthouse. ____

8 (a) The sun is a large **structure** made up of mostly gas. ____

(b) The **structure** was only half complete when the hurricane struck. ____

(c) Arlington's sports dome is the largest **structure** of its kind in the U.S. ____

(d) Milo wrote down the **structure** so that he wouldn't forget it. ____

10B Making Connections
Circle the letter next to the correct answer.

cable
cathedral
convey
device
freight
landmark
method
rod
shaft
structure

1 Which word goes with *church?*

(a) device　　(b) vessel　　(c) nursery　　(d) cathedral

2 Which word goes with *long* and *straight?*

(a) rod　　(b) hinge　　(c) container　　(d) freight

3 Which word goes with *coal mine?*

(a) device　　(b) luxury　　(c) spine　　(d) shaft

4 Which word goes with *bridge?*

(a) device　　(b) structure　　(c) gift　　(d) freight

5 Which word goes with *carry?*

(a) confess　　(b) defend　　(c) survey　　(d) convey

6 Which word goes with *toaster?*

(a) cable   (b) device   (c) rod   (d) shaft

7 Which word goes with the *White House?*

(a) landmark   (b) cathedral   (c) continent   (d) milestone

8 Which word goes with *truck?*

(a) dome   (b) club   (c) shaft   (d) freight

10C Using Context Clues

Circle the letter next to the word that correctly completes the sentence.

1 The _____ is made of many strands of steel and can hold two tons.

(a) freight   (b) shaft   (c) cable   (d) cocoon

2 The enormous _____ took two hundred years to build and was finished in 1345.

(a) chasm   (b) atlas   (c) freight   (d) cathedral

3 The invention of the airplane gave people a new _____ of getting around.

(a) device   (b) structure   (c) attitude   (d) method

4 The _____ was six feet long and had a diameter of half an inch.

(a) cathedral   (b) rod   (c) hinge   (d) chimney

5 Marcus came up with a _____ to the puzzle.

(a) structure   (b) device   (c) solution   (d) schedule

6 It took five minutes to reach the bottom of the _____.

(a) shaft   (b) rod   (c) attitude   (d) solution

7 The French castles were _____ built to last a long time.

(a) structures (b) devices (c) cathedrals (d) schedules

10D Completing Sentences

Circle each answer choice that correctly completes the sentence. Each question has three correct answers.

1 The wooden **rod**

(a) can have a flag attached to it.

(b) forms part of the kite.

(c) has six square sides with numbers on them.

(d) can be used as a fishing pole.

2 The **method**

(a) we were following was based on an old process.

(b) might have to be changed as we learn more.

(c) lay without being disturbed for a thousand years.

(d) can be done in just six easy steps.

3 **Freight**

(a) can be carried by plane, train, or ship.

(b) is usually in the form of air.

(c) prices can almost double during the summer months.

(d) is checked for explosives by dogs trained to sniff for them.

4 This **device**

(a) opens and closes the garage door.

(b) made it possible to see the craters on the Moon.

(c) was designed by a person who had trouble sleeping.

(d) can be grown almost anywhere and needs little watering.

cable
cathedral
convey
device
freight
landmark
method
rod
shaft
structure

5 The **cathedral**

    (a) holds over five hundred people.

    (b) is a special day of the year.

    (c) has some wonderful glass windows.

    (d) is the tallest building in the town.

6 I offered to **convey**

    (a) the air if it got too windy.

    (b) the children to the circus in my car.

    (c) the food to the event for half the price of what the others charge.

    (d) the message of hope to the city mayor.

10E Vocabulary in Context
Read the passage.

Life's Ups and Downs

    Skyscrapers are a common sight in the world's big cities. They have been with us, though, for only about 125 years. The first one was built in Chicago in 1885. It had ten stories. Let's discover what led to this new kind of building, which changed the shape of cities.

    • • • • • • • • • • • • •

    There used to be only one way to make very tall buildings. Stones were cut to the correct shape. Then the stones were placed one on top of the other. This is the way the great **cathedrals** of Europe were built hundreds of years ago. The enormous weight of the walls was spread over a large area on the ground. The base of the walls had to be many feet thick. This **method** of building used a large amount of cut stone. And stone was not cheap. That was one problem with tall buildings. Another was getting people from the ground to the higher levels. Most people were not willing to climb more than five flights of stairs.

The first problem was solved in the late 1880s. That is when steel came into wide use. A set of steel girders fastened together supported the **structure.** That way, the outside walls no longer carried the weight of the building. The walls could now be made of lighter materials. There was no limit to how tall buildings could be, except for all those stairs! Elisha Otis, a mechanic from Vermont, solved the second problem. In the 1850s, Otis was working in a factory that made beds. Elevators then were run by steam power. They were just coming into use in America. Their main purpose was to move **freight** from one factory floor to another. The place where Otis worked had one. It was just a cage hanging from a rope. It was raised or lowered inside a framework that kept it from swinging. If the rope broke, there was nothing to stop the cage from crashing to the ground.

Otis thought about this. He came up with a **device** that would keep such accidents from happening. It was a kind of brake for the cage. As soon as the rope or wire **cable** broke and the cage began to fall, a spring caused two steel **rods** to shoot out of the sides of the cage. These fitted into slots running the length of the elevator **shaft.** That kept the cage from falling any farther. Otis's invention worked well. So in 1854, he took it to New York to a special business fair for new inventions. He climbed into the elevator cage. Then the cage was raised as high as it would go. After a signal was given, a helper on the ground cut the rope holding up the cage. Instead of falling, the cage remained in place. The crowd gasped. Then they cheered. Otis began taking orders for the elevator company he started. The company still carries his name.

Otis's invention could be used to **convey** people safely to the upper floors of very tall buildings. This helped make the skyscraper possible. Elevators improved even more when they began running on electricity instead of steam. Electric elevators were faster, smoother, and quieter. They were also less likely to break down. The ten-story Chicago building, which was demolished in 1931, was followed by Manhattan's first skyscraper, the twenty-two-story

| cable |
| cathedral |
| convey |
| device |
| freight |
| landmark |
| method |
| rod |
| shaft |
| structure |

Flatiron Building. It is still a New York **landmark.** Then there is the 110-story Willis Tower in Chicago. It has over one hundred elevators. The fastest ones make the quarter-mile ride to the top in one minute with perfect safety.

Answer each of the following questions with a sentence. If a question does not contain a vocabulary word from the lesson's word list, use one in your answer. Use each word only once.

1 Give the names of some **devices** that enable people to reach the upper stories of buildings.

_____

_____

2 What kind of tall building was built before skyscrapers were invented?

_____

_____

3 What **method** was used to support the weight of tall buildings made of stone?

_____

_____

4 Why is 1854 a **landmark** in the history of tall buildings?

_____

_____

5 Which **structure** was New York City's first skyscraper?

_____

_____

6 Why were there no **cables** for electricity in the early elevators?

_____

_____

7 What keeps an elevator from moving side to side?

_____

_____

8 Why would the **rods** that Otis used have to be very strong?

_____

_____

9 What are some different uses of elevators?

_____

_____

10 If you were riding an elevator to the top of the Willis Tower in Chicago, how long would it take you?

_____

_____

Fun FACT

- As you learned in Lesson 7, **advice** is a noun that means "something that is given," and its verb form is _advise_. The same type of spelling change takes place in **device** and _devise_. _Device_ is a noun that means "something made or invented," and the verb form, _devise_, means "to make or invent something."

cable
cathedral
convey
device
freight
landmark
method
rod
shaft
structure

method

noun A way of doing something.

Academic Context

In math, one **method** for measuring length is to use a ruler.

Word Family

methodical (adjective)

methodically (adverb)

Discussion & Writing Prompt

You want to find out who is taller: you or your friend. What **method** would you use?

2 min.	3 min.
1. Turn and talk to your partner or group.	**2.** Write 1–3 sentences.
Use this space to take notes or draw your ideas.	Be ready to share what you have written.

Review

Hidden Message Write the word that is missing from each sentence in the boxes next to it. All the words are from Lessons X and X. The shaded boxes will answer the following riddle:

A bus driver made her way along a one-way street going toward the oncoming traffic. A police officer saw this, yet did nothing. Why?

1. This half-built _____ will soon be our new school.

2. This recipe gives a new _____ for cooking chicken.

3. My decision to quit the team is a fair one, and I will _____ it.

4. That crane with a long _____ will lift the steel beam.

5. Boil the potatoes in a(n) _____ of salt and water.

6. The opposite of happiness is _____.

7. Each iron _____ was three feet long

8. This timing _____ will turn on the lamp at night.

9. A smile is a clear way to _____ that you are friendly.

10. The _____ in Washington, D.C., is open to all people.

11. From the _____, we learned that most students like the school lunches.

12. The Space Needle is Seattle's best known _____.

13. The rescue workers entered the mine _____ carefully.

14. The slope here is so _____ you hardly notice it.

15. Breaking the new bicycle on purpose was an act of _____.

16. A cheerful _____ helps when you have problems.

17. If you can't guess the answer, I'll give you a(n) _____.

18. All of the trains on this line carry _____ only.

Study the words. Then do the exercises that follow.

diagram

n. A plan or drawing that shows how something works or how different parts fit together.

Ahmad quickly made a **diagram** of the stockroom showing us where he wanted each box placed.

frustrate

v. To keep from carrying out a plan or reaching a goal.

The foul weather today **frustrated** our plan to visit the zoo.

frustrating *adj.* Causing one to be upset or discouraged.

Seeing his favorite ball on the dresser just out of reach was very **frustrating** to Yves.

Tell your partner about something that frustrated a plan you made.

graduate

n. A person who has finished a course of study.

The **graduates** proudly walked up on stage to receive their diplomas.

v. To finish a course of study and receive a diploma.

After Sarah **graduated** from high school, she worked for a year to save money for college.

prank

n. A playful trick or joke.

As a **prank,** Melanie put a rubber snake in Mr. Donne's desk drawer.

primary

adj. 1. First in importance.

After the fire, Jenn's **primary** need was a place to stay.

2. First in order.

After **primary** school, we go on to middle school.

 . . . .

Talk to your partner about the primary person in your life.

risk

v. To take a chance on being hurt or losing something.

You **risk** being thrown from the car in an accident if you do not wear a seat belt.

n. The chance of getting hurt or suffering loss or failure.

We put on sunscreen to lower the **risk** of skin cancer.

risky *adj.* Likely to cause harm or damage; dangerous.

Mike did not think it was **risky** to ride a bike without a helmet until he fell off and bumped his head.

. . . .

Discuss with your partner what to do if you see someone doing something risky on the playground.

stress

v. To pay special attention to.

The dentist **stressed** the importance of brushing our teeth daily to keep them healthy.

n. 1. A strain or pressure put on a person or thing.

Although Renee enjoys being on the swim team, she also feels **stress** before each race.

2. Special force put on a word or part of a word.

When you say "cocoon," you place the **stress** on the second syllable.

 . . . .

Say your full name for your partner, putting stress on your first name.

urge

v. To speak strongly for something; to argue in favor of something.

Because we had liked the play at the children's theater so much, we **urged** our cousins to see it.

n. A strong feeling of wanting to do something; a strong wish.

Anna felt an **urge** to dive into the cool pond.

. . . .

Tell your partner about an urge you have.

vacant

adj. Having nothing or no one in it; not filled; empty.

As the children explored the second floor of the old castle, they found room after room completely **vacant.**

vigorous

adj. Demanding strength or energy; very active.

My grandparents enjoyed their **vigorous** hike in the White Mountains.

Words and Their Meanings

Look at the group of words next to the number. Then circle the letter next to the word that has the same meaning.

1 most important

(a) primary   (b) vacant   (c) frustrating   (d) vigorous

2 a playful trick

(a) risk   (b) diagram   (c) stress   (d) prank

3 to block a plan

(a) to urge   (b) to stress   (c) to frustrate   (d) to graduate

4 a strong desire

(a) urge   (b) graduate   (c) diagram   (d) risk

Look at the word next to the number. Then circle the letter next to the group of words that has the same meaning.

5 stress

(a) to write out in full   (b) to give special attention to

(c) to stay away from   (d) to make possible

6 vacant

(a) out of sight   (b) easily broken

(c) of limited use   (d) empty inside

7 risk

(a) to place a limit on   (b) to stay away from

(c) to take a chance   (d) to surprise or shock

8 graduate

(a) to take part in   (b) to complete a course of study

(c) to learn by heart   (d) to change slowly over time

diagram
frustrate
graduate
prank
primary
risk
stress
urge
vacant
vigorous

11B Just the Right Word

Replace each phrase in bold with a single word (or form of the word) from the word list.

1 Cecilia enjoys the karate class because it is **very active** exercise.

2 When the bridge was designed, the builders did not know it would have so much **strain or pressure put upon it** from big trucks.

3 All the **people who had finished the course of study** gathered for a group photograph.

4 Look in the box for the **drawing showing how the different parts fit in place,** which will help us put the bookcase together.

5 When the school bus was stopped in traffic for half an hour, it was **upsetting and discouraging** for both the driver and the students.

6 People say that there is more **chance of being hurt** when riding in a car than when riding in an airplane.

7 With the hurricane moving up the coast, Carrie is **speaking strongly in favor of the idea** that we leave the cottage right now to go to a shelter.

11c Applying Meanings

Circle the letter next to the correct answer.

1 Which of the following can be **vacant?**

(a) a crowded room   (b) a continent

(c) a hotel room   (d) an individual

2 Which of the following might be called a **prank?**

(a) eating lunch   (b) buying a puppy

(c) cheating on a test   (d) pretending to be someone else on the phone

3 Who will you find in the **primary** grades in school?

(a) first through third graders   (b) seventh through ninth graders

(c) fourth through sixth graders   (d) tenth through twelfth graders

4 Which of the following would you probably use to make a **diagram?**

(a) a chain   (b) a pencil

(c) a brick   (d) a container

5 When do you expect to be **vigorous?**

(a) when you are hungry   (b) while sleeping

(c) when you are thirsty   (d) while doing exercises

6 Which of the following can be **risky?**

(a) walking near a very busy road   (b) taking a nap

(c) memorizing a poem   (d) finding a quarter

7 How might you **frustrate** a robbery?

(a) write a letter   (b) do your homework

(c) call the police   (d) go on a vacation

diagram
frustrate
graduate
prank
primary
risk
stress
urge
vacant
vigorous

11D

Word Study: Latin Roots

Complete each sentence with a word chosen from this or an earlier lesson. The number after each space gives the lesson the word is from. You might want to review the information about roots in Lesson 7, Exercise 7D.

1 The Latin *primus* means "first." It forms the root of the word _____ (11), which means "first in importance."

2 The Latin *malus* means "bad." It forms the root of the word _____ (9), which means "the wish to hurt others on purpose."

3 The Latin *vacere* means "to be empty." It forms the root of the word _____ (11), which means "having nothing or no one in it."

4 The Latin *structus* means "built." It forms the root of the word _____ (10), which means "something that is built."

5 The Latin *vigere* means "to be lively." It forms the root of the word _____ (11), which means "very active."

11E

Vocabulary in Context
Read the passage.

Meet a Firefighter

Fighting fires is dangerous work. Have you ever met a firefighter? Kristin Hartman, who was born and raised in Calgary, Canada, fights fires for a living. Let's discover more about her and her job.

· · · · · · · · · · · · ·

When Kristin Hartman was growing up, she enjoyed **vigorous** exercise, such as hiking, skiing, and rock climbing. She wanted to be a physical-education teacher. Then, hearing that the local fire department had some positions **vacant,** she changed her mind. The training course lasted eight weeks. Kristin **graduated,** along with thirty-three men. She then joined the Calgary Fire Department, which had almost one thousand firefighters. She was the fourth woman to be hired.

Kristin often visits schools to talk about her job and about how to prevent fires. When students ask her what sort of person makes a good firefighter, she tells them, "You must be comfortable with heights and prepared to **risk** your life." She also **stresses** the importance of fitness. A firefighter has to have strength and energy. Firefighters should also be able to stay calm. In a fire, many things are happening at once. There may be people in the building or things that can explode. Each fire is different. The firefighters work together closely and depend on each other for support.

Four out of five fires start in the home. Kristin **urges** students to be careful around the house. Here are some of the things she tells them. Never play with matches. They are not toys. Keep space heaters away from things that can burn, such as curtains. Do not wear loose clothing when cooking at the kitchen stove or on a grill. Kristin explains that a wood or paper fire can be stopped with water but not one started with fat or grease. Water only spreads the fire. To stop a grease fire, cover the pan with a lid. This cuts off the air and stops the burning.

The **primary** cause of death in a fire is breathing in smoke. That is why smoke alarms are so important. You should check them at least once a month to make sure they are working. Kristin tells students to sleep with the bedroom door closed. If a fire starts, it will hold back heat and smoke. If the door feels hot, do not open it. Leave by another way such as a window. In addition, you should have an escape plan. Make a **diagram** of your home. Show at least two ways out of each room. Make sure that everyone living in the house or staying there understands it. Then, agree on a place outdoors where everyone can gather to be counted. When firefighters arrive, they want to know whether anyone is in the house and needs to be rescued.

diagram
frustrate
graduate
prank
primary
risk
stress
urge
vacant
vigorous

What is the most **frustrating** part of Kristin's job? The answer is easy. It is rushing to put out a fire only to find it is a false alarm. Often these calls happen by accident; no one can be blamed. But sometimes a person will set off an alarm as a **prank.** This is a dangerous and foolish joke. The person doing it can cause a great amount of trouble. Somewhere a real fire may be burning, but the firefighters cannot go because they have been called out on a false alarm.

Answer each of the following questions with a sentence. If a question does not contain a vocabulary word from the lesson's word list, use one in your answer. Use each word only once.

1 What is the **primary** thing to remember about matches?

_____

_____

2 Why is it a good idea to sleep with the bedroom door closed?

_____

_____

3 How can a **diagram** of your home help you when there is a fire?

_____

_____

4 Why do firefighters need to be fit and strong?

_____

_____

5 How many other women **graduated** with Kristin?

_____

_____

6 What effect would a traffic jam have on firefighters going to a fire?

_____

_____

7 Why should you fight the **urge** to throw water on a grease fire?

_____

_____

8 What must the firefighters wonder when the alarm rings?

_____

_____

9 What are two things that you think might cause **stress** in firefighters?

_____

_____

10 Why do firefighters need to know if a burning house is **vacant?**

_____

_____

Fun FACT

- **Vacant** comes from the Latin term that also gave us the word _vacation_. So when the school building is _vacant_, or empty of people, it is because you are on your summer _vacation!_

diagram
frustrate
graduate
prank
primary
risk
stress
urge
vacant
vigorous

primary

adjective First in order or the most important.

Word Family

prime (adjective)

primarily (adverb)

Context Clues

These sentences give clues to the meaning of **primary.**

> Our **primary** needs are water, food, and a safe place to live.

> Not brushing your teeth is a **primary** cause of cavities.

Discussion & Writing Prompt

Why do you think elementary school is also called **primary** school?

2 min.	3 min.
1. Turn and talk to your partner or group.	2. Write 1–3 sentences.
Use this space to take notes or draw your ideas.	Be ready to share what you have written.

Study the words. Then do the exercises that follow.

adopt

v. 1. To take into one's home and to raise a child as part of one's family.

The Beckwiths were happy to **adopt** both the brother and sister so that the children could stay together.

2. To take up and make one's own.

Our town **adopted** a new recycling plan.

Talk with your partner about a good habit you want to adopt.

arouse

v. 1. To awaken from sleep.

Tanya was **aroused** in the night by her dog's barking.

2. To excite or bring about.

Our visit to Gettysburg last summer **aroused** my brother's interest in the Civil War.

arrange

v. 1. To put in a certain order.

Marta and Vincent **arranged** the desks and chairs in three long rows before the students arrived.

2. To plan or prepare.

Eli **arranged** to meet us at the train station at 1:30.

Work with your partner to arrange your pencils from largest to smallest.

cell

n. 1. A small room with little or no furniture, especially one used for prisoners.

Each jail **cell** had only a bunk bed, a sink, and a toilet.

2. A tiny unit of living matter.

Plant **cells** can be seen only by using a microscope.

3. A small enclosed space grouped with others.

The **cells** of a honeycomb have six sides.

infection

n. A disease caused by germs.

You should clean that cut carefully to prevent **infection.**

influence

n. 1. The power to cause change or bring about certain results.

The **influence** of Martin Luther King Jr.'s ideas was clear in the marchers' peaceful actions.

2. Someone or something that can cause change.

Listening to tapes of the famous young violin player had a great **influence** on Lydia's playing.

v. To cause change or bring about certain results.

The position of the moon in relation to Earth **influences** tides around the world.

Tell your partner about someone who has had a good influence on you.

injure

v. To do harm to; to hurt or damage.

Acid rain, which is a result of burning coal, **injures** plants, soil, and water.

injury *n.* Harm or damage.

Jonathan's fall on the ice is what caused his wrist **injury.**

 Talk to your partner about an injury you had.

pattern

n. 1. The way in which shapes, objects, or colors are placed in relation to each other.

The circular **pattern** of the garden was clear when I looked at it from the balcony.

2. A plan or diagram that is used as a guide for making things.

Caitlyn used this paper **pattern** to cut out the pieces for a jacket.

series

n. A number of similar things laid out or happening in a certain order.

This summer, the **series** of evening concerts by the river includes one of my favorite guitar players.

 Tell your partner about a series of dreams you had.

vision

n. 1. Eyesight; the sense of sight.

After he was fitted with suitable glasses, Simon's **vision** improved greatly.

2. Something imagined or hoped for; a dream of what might be.

The people in the town had a **vision** of a river clean enough to swim in, and they worked for years to make it happen.

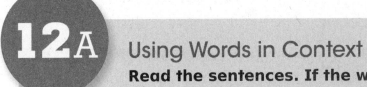

Using Words in Context

Read the sentences. If the word in bold is used correctly, write C on the line. If the word is used incorrectly, write I on the line.

1 (a) There was a **pattern** of blue and white stripes on the blanket. _____

(b) **Patterns** grow best against a wall with lots of sunshine. _____

(c) The dress **pattern** was printed on paper and was easy to follow. _____

(d) Blow the **pattern** on the water over to me. _____

2 (a) Martin Luther King Jr. had a **vision** of a world where all people are equal. _____

(b) The best way to create a **vision** is to open your arms wide. _____

(c) Pull back your **vision** so we can see your face. _____

(d) The new pair of glasses greatly improved my **vision.** _____

3 (a) She decided on her own without any outside **influence.** _____

(b) An attack of **influence** kept her in bed for a week. _____

(c) My teacher has **influenced** me by making me want to learn. _____

(d) The weather will **influence** whether the soccer game will be postponed. _____

4 (a) Everything in the store window had been **arranged** perfectly. _____

(b) Aunt Eunice **arranged** for the twins to share the extra bedroom. _____

(c) Prices **arranged** from under ten dollars to over a thousand. _____

(d) We **arranged** to meet at noon under the town clock. _____

5 (a) The car struck us from behind but caused no **injuries.** ____

(b) Skipping classes **injures** your chances of getting good grades. ____

(c) The pyramids of Egypt have **injured** for four thousand years. ____

(d) I didn't mean to **injure** Kate's feelings when I complained about the food. ____

6 (a) The guard opened the **cell** door to let the prisoner out. ____

(b) Brain **cells** are called neurons and do all our thinking. ____

(c) The **cells** in the honeycomb are made from wax. ____

(d) I told him he could **cell** the bike or give it away. ____

7 (a) Olivia **adopted** a pair of sandals. ____

(b) Think carefully before you **adopt** a stray animal. ____

(c) The Keegans **adopted** the local way of dressing after they arrived. ____

(d) The device can be **adopted** to run on batteries. ____

8 (a) He wasn't being **series** when he said you wouldn't be welcome. ____

(b) A **series** of banging sounds made me think my little sister had woken up. ____

(c) A new cartoon **series** is starting on TV tonight. ____

(d) The password was a **series** of different numbers and letters. ____

| adopt |
| arouse |
| arrange |
| cell |
| infection |
| influence |
| injure |
| pattern |
| series |
| vision |

12B Making Connections

Circle the letter next to the correct answer.

1 Which word goes with *awaken?*
(a) injure   (b) arrange   (c) adopt   (d) arouse

2 Which word goes with a *cut?*
(a) influence   (b) infection   (c) cell   (d) vision

3 Which word goes with *put on display?*
(a) adopt   (b) arrange   (c) influence   (d) injure

4 Which word goes with *causing change?*
(a) amaze   (b) influence   (c) arrange   (d) convey

5 Which word goes with *hurt?*
(a) vision   (b) cell   (c) injury   (d) influence

6 Which word goes with the numbers *2, 4, 6, 8?*
(a) infection   (b) series   (c) primary   (d) device

7 Which word goes with *eyesight?*
(a) pattern   (b) influence   (c) story   (d) vision

8 Which word goes with *take up?*
(a) arouse   (b) arrange   (c) adopt   (d) frustrate

Using Context Clues
Circle the letter next to the word that correctly completes the sentence.

1 The sudden noise _____ me from a sound sleep.

(a) adopted   (b) arranged   (c) aroused   (d) influenced

2 The _____ is the tiny thing that makes up all life.

(a) vision   (b) pattern   (c) cell   (d) device

3 The _____ of dots repeats itself every ten inches around the curtains.

(a) cell   (b) pattern   (c) vision   (d) diagram

4 Padma had a(n) _____ that she would be a police officer when she grew up.

(a) diagram   (b) injury   (c) pattern   (d) vision

5 Sammy hoped I would _____ one of the kittens.

(a) adopt   (b) arrange   (c) arouse   (d) influence

6 To prevent _____, keep a bandage over the cut.

(a) vision   (b) infection   (c) influence   (d) malice

7 The _____ shows how the engine works.

(a) cell   (b) pattern   (c) influence   (d) diagram

adopt
arouse
arrange
cell
infection
influence
injure
pattern
series
vision

12D Completing Sentences

Circle each answer choice that correctly completes the sentence. Each question has three correct answers.

1 We were **aroused**

(a) from a nap at five o'clock.

(b) by the speech the mayor made.

(c) to help us go to sleep.

(d) every morning with a knock on the door.

2 He can **arrange**

(a) the blocks in any order you like.

(b) for you to stay with his sister.

(c) for you to get free tickets to the concert.

(d) you into a corner.

3 Each **cell**

(a) in a honeycomb fits neatly against those around it.

(b) has two beds and a sink.

(c) in the plant worked to keep it alive.

(d) has to be signed by the president for it to become law.

4 **Infection**

(a) can be prevented by washing your hands.

(b) is mostly sugar and should be avoided.

(c) is caused by germs.

(d) can spread quickly if not treated.

5 The **influence**

(a) of the athlete has been very great.

(b) of gravity can be felt every second.

(c) of the two rivers forms Lake Wobegon.

(d) that the past has on the present is important.

6 The **pattern**

(a) on my notebook was drawn by my best friend.

(b) told me to turn out the light.

(c) is a copy of a design from my favorite comic book.

(d) is easy for a beginner to follow.

7 A **series**

(a) of mystery books is all we talk about after school.

(b) of letters and numbers gives you the password.

(c) of only one coin was on the floor.

(d) of e-mails was sent, all saying the same thing.

8 Did you **injure**

(a) your room like I asked you to?

(b) your knee when you fell on the sidewalk?

(c) that woman when you stepped on her foot?

(d) your father with a rude comment about his shirt?

12E Vocabulary in Context
Read the passage.

adopt
arouse
arrange
cell
infection
influence
injure
pattern
series
vision

Reading with the Fingertips

Have you ever noticed the raised dots that label some elevators and public restrooms? This is a method of writing that enables people who cannot see to read by using their fingertips. Its name is Braille. Let's discover how this form of writing came into use. First, we must learn about its inventor.

• • • • • • • • • • • • •

Louis Braille was born in France in 1809. He was the son of a saddle maker. When he was three, he **injured** an eye in an accident in his father's workshop. The **infection** from the wound spread to his other eye. Within a year he lost his **vision.** When he was ten, he was sent to a school for the blind. The school was in Paris. The students there learned by listening to their teachers.

One day, a visitor came to the school. His name was Charles Barbier. He was to have an enormous **influence** on Braille. Louis was then twelve years old. Barbier had invented a new way of writing. He had hoped the French army would **adopt** his method. This writing was designed to be used at night. Soldiers could read it without showing a light. Barbier hoped the head of the school whose students lived their lives in darkness could use his way of writing.

Louis Braille stood out among those students. His mind was quick. He was eager to learn. The head of school invited him to meet the visitor. Barbier began to show how his writing worked. Braille's interest was **aroused.** Barbier took a sheet of thick paper. Using a pointed instrument, he punched a **series** of holes in it without going through. This caused raised dots to appear on the other side of the paper. These dots were grouped together in **cells.** The cells could be placed in any of twelve positions. Each group stood for a different sound. By running a fingertip over them, a person could read a message.

Braille was excited by Barbier's invention. But he knew that it needed to be simpler. He started working on it at once. Instead of twelve positions for each unit, he decided to work with six. This let a reader make sense of the raised dots more quickly and easily.

To understand Louis Braille's method, picture a dice with the six dots showing. Each of the two rows of three dots is going from top to bottom. The dots in Braille are formed in this **pattern.** A single raised dot in the top left position is the letter *A*. Two dots, one at top left and one at center left, form the letter *B*. There are sixty-three ways to **arrange** these dots. That way they can stand for other things besides the twenty-six letters of the alphabet. For example, a single dot at center left is a comma.

Braille remained at the school all his life. He taught there. He also helped to print books that used his method. He played the organ there, too. Braille was a very good musician. He showed people how to write music in Braille.

Charles Barbier did not sell his method to the army. But he played a part in changing forever the way blind people read. Because of what he started and Louis Braille completed, people everywhere who cannot see are no longer limited by blindness. They can read from one hundred to two hundred words a minute. That is about the same speed as most people who use their eyes to read.

Answer each of the following questions with a sentence. If a question does not contain a vocabulary word from the lesson's word list, use one in your answer. Use each word only once.

1 What is one step in the **series** of events that led to Braille's invention?

_____

_____

2 How was Louis Braille able to meet Barbier?

_____

_____

3 What **vision** did Barbier have for his invention?

_____

_____

4 How did Barbier and Braille's methods of writing differ?

_____

_____

5 Why did Barbier show his idea to the head of the school for the blind?

_____

_____

| adopt |
| arouse |
| arrange |
| cell |
| infection |
| influence |
| injure |
| pattern |
| series |
| vision |

6 How did Louis Braille **influence** the lives of blind people?

_____

_____

7 Was Braille blind from birth? Explain your answer.

_____

_____

8 Why did Braille lose sight in both eyes?

_____

_____

9 Why was Braille's method of writing **adopted** while Barbier's was not?

_____

_____

10 How do blind people become aware of the **pattern** of dots?

_____

_____

Fun FACT

· ·

- **Series** is spelled the same in its singular and plural forms. The baseball _series_ is on. Two new television _series_ begin in May.

series

noun A number of similar things that happen in order.

Academic Context

In math, 1, 3, 5, 7, 9, 11 . . . is a **series** of odd numbers. Can you think of another **series** of numbers you have learned about in math?

Discussion & Writing Prompt

A **series** of storybooks tells different stories about the same characters. A TV **series** is a set of television shows about the same characters. Tell about your favorite book or TV **series**.

2 min.	3 min.
1. Turn and talk to your partner or group.	2. Write 1–3 sentences.
Use this space to take notes or draw your ideas.	Be ready to share what you have written.

Review

Lessons 11 & 12

Crossword Puzzle Solve the puzzle by writing the missing word in each sentence in the boxes with the matching numbers. All the words are from Lessons 11 and 12.

ACROSS

4. Could you _____ these roses in a vase before the party begins?

5. This _____ shows where to oil the machine.

7. Do you think this book on soccer will _____ Angela's interest?

10. Pretending to be sick seemed like a harmless _____, but it caused trouble.

11. These new glasses will improve your _____.

14. The _____ of being hurt is low.

15. Today's rain will _____ our plans for a hike in the woods.

17. Brock has read every book in this mystery _____.

18. The Yangs plan to _____ a second child.

19. Austin's polite manners were a good _____ on his rude cousin.

DOWN

1. Timber is one of the _____ products that Canada sells.

2. After a(n) _____ swim, Luz rested on a towel.

3. I fought the _____ to scratch my bug bites.

6. Keep the cut clean so there is no _____.

8. Ice on the front steps could cause a(n) _____.

9. What will the twins do when they _____ from high school?

11. The apartment next door has been _____ since the Bergs moved out.

12. To say the word *forget,* you place the _____ on second part.

13. Her favorite skirt was the one with a(n) _____ of tiny yellow flowers on white.

16. The small, plain room looked like a(n) _____ in a prison.

Wordly Wise 3000 • Book 3   **143**

Study the words. Then do the exercises that follow.

calendar

> *n.* A chart or diagram showing the days, weeks, and months of the year in order.
>
> On the wall **calendar** in the kitchen, Jodie circled the day of the picnic in red.

carnival

> *n.* A fair or show with food stalls, parades, rides, and other ways to have fun.
>
> The police are directing traffic away from Center Street where the **carnival** is set up and ready to begin.

experience

> *n.* 1. Knowledge or skill that comes from having done certain things.
>
> Panthea had **experience** caring for plants and offered to take care of Mrs. Levy's garden.
>
> 2. Something that happens to a person; an event in one's life.
>
> Jubilee said that taking part in the Olympics was an **experience** she would never forget.
>
> *v.* To have happen to; to go through something.
>
> Marcelo **experienced** only a tiny pain when the nurse stuck the needle in his arm.

Tell your partner about a great experience in your life.

govern

> *v.* To be in charge of; to control or rule.
>
> Most people in the city like the way the mayor **governs** it.

Discuss with your partner how your teacher governs your class.

gulf

n. 1. A large area of a sea or ocean that is partly enclosed by land.

The **Gulf** of Mexico is bordered to the north and east by the United States and to the west and south by Mexico.

2. A great distance between.

After their argument, Sharin felt that a **gulf** had opened between her and her friend.

Show your partner how you can make a gulf between your feet.

haste

n. Speed in acting or moving.

Roosevelt left for school in such **haste** that he forgot his backpack.

hasty *adj.* Done or made quickly without careful thought.

When the rain started falling heavily, the crowd at the outdoor concert made a **hasty** dash to their cars.

nation

n. 1. A place with borders and its own leaders; a single country.

South Sudan, a country in Africa, became a **nation** in 2011.

2. The people of a single country.

The Prime Minister of Canada will speak to the **nation** at nine o'clock this evening.

national *adj.* Of or belonging to the people of a single country.

Labor Day, which comes on the first Monday of September, is a **national** holiday in the United States.

Tell your partner your favorite national holiday.

scatter

v. 1. To throw here and there; to spread about.

Lucy likes to **scatter** the feed for her chickens.

2. To move quickly in different directions.

When Carlos covered his eyes and started counting slowly to thirty, the rest of the children **scattered** to the best hiding places they could find.

surrender

v. To give in or give up; to accept defeat.

The soldiers raised a white flag over the fort to stop the attack, and then they **surrendered.**

Show your partner how someone who has surrendered might look.

thrill

n. A feeling of joy or excitement.

At the museum, my biggest **thrill** was seeing the skeleton of Sue, the largest and most complete dinosaur of its kind yet discovered.

v. To feel or cause to feel joy or excitement.

The memory of shaking hands with the famous boxer Muhammad Ali **thrilled** Maggie.

13A Words and Their Meanings

Look at the group of words next to the number. Then circle the letter next to the word that has the same meaning.

1 a feeling of great joy

(a) thrill   (b) gulf   (c) carnival   (d) calendar

2 to spread around

    (a) experience   (b) scatter   (c) govern   (d) surrender

3 a great space between

    (a) experience   (b) haste   (c) nation   (d) gulf

4 speed in doing something

    (a) haste   (b) carnival   (c) nation   (d) calendar

Look at the word next to the number. Then circle the letter next to the group of words that has the same meaning.

5 experience

    (a) to look forward to   (b) to live through something

    (c) to offer advice   (d) to have no knowledge of

6 govern

    (a) to fail and try again   (b) to blame others

    (c) to control or rule   (d) to blame oneself

7 surrender

    (a) to give up   (b) to move to one side

    (c) to stay on   (d) to go straight

8 nation

    (a) the people of the world   (b) the people living in cities

    (c) the people living outside of cities   (d) the people of one country

13B Just the Right Word

Replace each phrase in bold with a single word (or form of the word) from the word list.

1 After working at the racetrack last summer, Ivan has a great deal of **knowledge and skill** with horses.

2 Tobias decided to dress up as a clown for the **fair that will have a parade with people wearing fancy costumes.**

3 Our teacher's advice before the test was to read carefully and to not be **quick in making up our mind** about choosing the answers.

4 The **chart showing the days, weeks, and months of the year** says that April 4 falls on a Monday.

5 The pigeons near the fountain **flew off in all directions** when the children came running nearby.

6 In 1919, the Grand Canyon was named a park that belonged to the **people of this country.**

7 The Irish dancers **brought great excitement to** us with their amazing skill and beautiful movements.

| calendar |
| carnival |
| experience |
| govern |
| gulf |
| haste |
| nation |
| scatter |
| surrender |
| thrill |

13C Applying Meanings

Circle the letter next to the correct answer.

1 Which of the following can be **governed?**
(a) an ocean
(b) a country
(c) a star
(d) an accident

2 How would you use a **calendar?**
(a) to tell the time
(b) to read the news
(c) to find out the date
(d) to learn the temperature

3 Which of the following is a **nation?**
(a) Mexico
(b) Mexico City
(c) California
(d) Washington, D.C.

4 When are people likely to **surrender?**
(a) when they are sleeping
(b) when no one is chasing them
(c) when all is at peace
(d) when they cannot escape

5 Which of the following can be **scattered?**
(a) pebbles
(b) rivers
(c) highways
(d) infections

6 Where would you look for a **gulf?**
(a) in a phone book
(b) on a schedule
(c) in an atlas
(d) in a diary

7 Which of the following can **experience** something?
(a) a schedule
(b) an urge
(c) a chasm
(d) an individual

13D Word Study: Synonyms

Look at each group of three words. Decide which two of the words are synonyms and circle them.

In Lesson 9 you learned that synonyms are words with the same or almost the same meaning. *Rich* and *wealthy* are synonyms.

1. prank   trick   carnival

2. dangerous   risky   amazing

3. empty   suitable   vacant

4. frustrating   vigorous   active

5. awaken   arouse   adopt

6. injure   arrange   harm

7. rule   thrill   govern

8. hasty   hurried   tired

calendar
carnival
experience
govern
gulf
haste
nation
scatter
surrender
thrill

Viva Cinco de Mayo

Mexican Americans enjoy the July Fourth holiday along with everyone else in the United States. But they also have a special holiday. It is May Fifth, Cinco de Mayo [sin´ ko day ma´ yoh]. Let's discover what happened on that date in 1862.

. . . .

Spanish rule over Mexico ended in 1821. The southern part of the country broke into several pieces. These became the countries of Central America. A war with the United States followed in 1848, which Mexico lost. The United States took all of the land north of the Rio Grande. Fourteen years later, Napoleon the Third, the ruler of France, decided to take what was left. He planned to make Mexico part of the French empire. Napoleon felt sure that he could succeed. He sent an army across the Atlantic Ocean. It landed at Veracruz on the **Gulf** of Mexico.

The French expected little trouble. After all, the country was now much smaller and weaker. The spirit of the Mexican people was low. They did not have a well-trained army. The French soldiers had many guns. They also had much more **experience** at fighting. The Mexicans, however, were not going to **surrender** without a struggle. In great **haste,** the Mexican leader General Zaragoza put together an army. When the French reached the town of Puebla, after marching 150 miles from the coast, Zaragoza's army was waiting. The date was May 5, 1862.

Zaragoza had fewer soldiers and only a small number of guns. He wasted no time in attacking, though. The battle lasted two hours. Zaragoza **scattered** the French soldiers; they ran for their lives. The Mexican people were **thrilled.** They had been pushed around for too long by other countries. They needed a victory. Now they had one. Even though Napoleon sent a much larger army the next year and defeated the Mexicans, this did not dim the pride that they had felt on May 5. By beating the French in battle, Mexico was telling the world that it had become a **nation.** It was no longer willing to be part of anyone's empire. In fact, the French rule lasted only until 1867. Napoleon's dream of adding to his empire ended. The Mexican people were at last left to **govern** themselves.

That is the story of May Fifth, a special date on the Mexican **calendar.** It is a day enjoyed by the people of Mexico and by all those with ties to that country. Bands play, and markets and food stalls sell many different delicious snacks. People can watch dancing displays or can take part in different games. Nowhere, however, do they have more fun than in the Mexican town of Puebla. There, during the **carnival,** people dress up like French and Mexican soldiers. Then they act out a pretend battle just like the one on May 5. In the end, the Mexican soldiers always win.

Answer each of the following questions with a sentence. If a question does not contain a vocabulary word from the lesson's word list, use one in your answer. Use each word only once.

. . . .

1 Is it correct to say that Napoleon the Third acted in a **hasty** way after his first army lost to Zaragoza? Explain your answer.

_____

_____

2 Which two **nations** were fighting each other at Puebla in 1862?

_____

_____

3 Who was in charge of Mexico until 1821?

_____

_____

4 Why was winning the battle on May 5, 1862, such an important **experience** for the Mexicans?

_____

_____

| calendar |
| carnival |
| experience |
| govern |
| gulf |
| haste |
| nation |
| scatter |
| surrender |
| thrill |

5 In 1848, in the war between Mexico and the United States, which side **surrendered?**

_____

_____

6 How did the battle at Puebla end?

_____

_____

7 Where do many Mexicans go to remember Cinco de Mayo?

_____

_____

8 How is the word _May_ written in a Mexican **calendar?**

_____

_____

9 Which part of the Cinco de Mayo holiday would you find **thrilling?**

_____

_____

10 Where did the French army land in 1862?

_____

_____

Fun FACT

- Many **carnivals** take place just before Lent, a time when some people do not eat any meat. The word comes from the Italian _carnelevare_, meaning "to remove the meat."

13 Vocabulary Extension

nation

noun A single country.

noun The people who live in a country.

Word Family

inter**nation**al (adjective)

national (adjective)

nationalism (noun)

Discussion & Writing Prompt

Name some things that make you think of your **nation.**

2 min.	3 min.
1. Turn and talk to your partner or group.	**2.** Write 1–3 sentences.
Use this space to take notes or draw your ideas.	Be ready to share what you have written.

Study the words. Then do the exercises that follow.

bold

adj. Showing little or no fear; ready to take risks.

Sarita's **bold** plan was to dress as a boy to try out for the male lead in the play.

 Tell your partner about one bold thing you have done.

cunning

adj. Clever at tricking others; sly.

No matter what we did, the raccoon found **cunning** ways to enter the garden for the corn.

n. Cleverness at tricking or fooling others.

Gretel's **cunning** saved her and Hansel from being cooked in the oven by the old witch.

deed

n. 1. Something done; an act.

Charlotte felt she had certainly done her good **deed** for the day when all the dishes were washed and dried.

2. A paper that shows who owns a certain building or piece of land.

The **deed** for the farm shows that the Saroto family has owned this land for at least one hundred years.

 Tell your partner about one good deed someone did for you.

doze

v. To sleep lightly; to nap.

Sabrina tiptoed quickly through the room so that she did not arouse Grandma, who was **dozing** in her chair.

jagged

adj. Having sharp points and edges; rough.

Be careful when you pick up the broken glass because the pieces are **jagged.**

positive

adj. 1. Certain; sure.

When you are **positive** you have finished the whole exercise, please give it to me.

2. Trying to make things better; useful.

Our teacher gave us some **positive** comments on the skit we were practicing for parents' night.

 Say something positive to your partner.

respect

v. To look up to; to have a high opinion of.

My friend **respected** the way I defended my views, even though she disagreed with them.

n. A good opinion of the worth or value of something.

Dad says he does not have **respect** for people who lie.

 Talk to your partner about a person you respect.

responsible

adj. 1. Being the cause of something.

Luke quickly explained to his parents that his dog, not he, was **responsible** for breaking the vase.

2. Trustworthy; reliable.

My aunt and uncle are looking for a **responsible** teenager to care for my cousins after school.

 Discuss with your partner how you could be a more responsible student at home.

smuggle

v. To carry in or bring out in a secret way.

The thieves **smuggled** the painting away from the museum in an ice-cream truck.

version

n. A story or account of something that may differ from other accounts of the same event.

Trying to find out how the accident happened was not easy, because the three people who saw it each gave a different **version** of what took place.

14A Using Words in Context

Read the sentences. If the word in bold is used correctly, write C on the line. If the word is used incorrectly, write I on the line.

❶ (a) A strip of **cunning** ran around the border. _____

(b) They are **cunning** themselves if they expect Cedric to change. _____

(c) Because of their **cunning,** wild foxes are hard to trap. _____

(d) Omar's **cunning** saved them all from having to do homework. _____

❷ (a) The **deeds** of the famous king have been known for years. _____

(b) The **deeds** had to be rebuilt after the hurricane struck. _____

(c) The **deeds** to the houses are kept in a safe place. _____

(d) The **deeds** bent in the wind. _____

❸ (a) "There is a **positive** side to everything," said Caleb. _____

(b) It was easier to come down the **positive** side of the mountain. _____

(c) The food was **positive,** but there was little of it. _____

(d) I think it happened ten days ago, but I can't be **positive.** _____

4 (a) The house has to be **respected** before the new people move in. _____

(b) Children learn to show **respect** for older people. _____

(c) It is our duty to **respect** the rights of others. _____

(d) Bowing to the queen is a sign of **respect.** _____

5 (a) We are all **responsible** for taking good care of the planet we call home. _____

(b) A six-year-old is not **responsible** enough to be left alone in the house. _____

(c) Players raised a **responsible** amount of cash for the hospital. _____

(d) The person **responsible** for the robbery admitted his guilt to the police. _____

6 (a) The puppies like to **smuggle** up against each other. _____

(b) Jonah was caught trying to **smuggle** food into the library. _____

(c) Sue offered us a plate of **smuggles** that she'd baked herself. _____

(d) The thieves **smuggled** the painting from the museum. _____

7 (a) I was feeling **jagged** after the game, so I rested for an hour. _____

(b) The glass bowl broke into dozens of **jagged** pieces. _____

(c) I explained that a few **jagged** edges needed to be smoothed. _____

(d) Stay close to shore and away from those **jagged** rocks. _____

8 (a) John Adams's **versions** to his wife were written down and kept by her. _____

(b) There are three different **versions** of what happened. _____

(c) I was reading from the children's **version** of the huge novel. _____

(d) On our way down, we took a different **version,** even though it took longer. _____

bold
cunning
deed
doze
jagged
positive
respect
responsible
smuggle
version

Making Connections
Circle the letter next to the correct answer.

1 Which word goes with *takes risks?*
(a) responsible   (b) positive   (c) cunning   (d) bold

2 Which word goes with *sleep?*
(a) respect   (b) doze   (c) adopt   (d) smuggle

3 Which word goes with *an act?*
(a) deed   (b) respect   (c) version   (d) jagged

4 Which word goes with *sure about something?*
(a) responsible   (b) cunning   (c) positive   (d) influence

5 Which word goes with *trustworthy?*
(a) responsible   (b) cunning   (c) bold   (d) hasty

6 Which word goes with *look up to?*
(a) arouse   (b) smuggle   (c) doze   (d) respect

7 Which word goes with *clever?*
(a) cunning   (b) positive   (c) responsible   (d) vigorous

Using Context Clues
Circle the letter next to the word that correctly completes the sentence.

1 Sammy made a _____ move and won the game.
(a) jagged   (b) responsible   (c) vigorous   (d) bold

2 I took a picture of Jenna _____ on the couch.
(a) smuggling   (b) dozing   (c) gusting   (d) relying

3 The _____ outline of mountain peaks stood out against the sky.
(a) vacant   (b) cunning   (c) positive   (d) jagged

4 It's against the law to _____ animals into the country.
(a) respect   (b) dangle   (c) smuggle   (d) attract

5 Malik's _____ of what happened was different than Josiah's.
(a) pattern   (b) series   (c) deed   (d) version

6 The award is given for only the bravest _____.
(a) visions   (b) injuries   (c) versions   (d) deeds

7 The firefighters who risk their lives have earned our _____.
(a) cunning   (b) respect   (c) infection   (d) influence

bold
cunning
deed
doze
jagged
positive
respect
responsible
smuggle
version

14D Completing Sentences

Circle each answer choice that correctly completes the sentence. Each question has three correct answers.

1 It will take a **bold**

(a) vision to win the votes.

(b) person to talk to the principal.

(c) effort on everyone's part.

(d) container to hold everything.

2 His **cunning**

(a) words were very intelligent.

(b) brain could always come up with something funny.

(c) infection took several weeks to heal.

(d) book sold one million copies.

3 The **jagged**

(a) pieces of glass should be picked up carefully.

(b) poem was exciting for students to read.

(c) hole in the side of the boat could not be repaired.

(d) edges of the rip were sewn together.

4 A **responsible**

(a) device is one that is easily fixed.

(b) person is the one who takes care of the problem.

(c) reporter tries to always tell the truth.

(d) person is one who always follows the rules.

5 A **positive**

(a) message is one of hope.

(b) person is one who is cheerful.

(c) injury is one that is serious.

(d) move is one that makes you feel happy.

© SSI • DO NOT DUPLICATE

Wordly Wise 3000 • Book 3   **161**

6 To **smuggle**

(a) with a stuffed animal is warm and comfortable.

(b) a phone into the classroom is foolish.

(c) secret plans to the enemy is wrong.

(d) candy into the movie theater is risky.

Vocabulary in Context
Read the passage.

Jason and the Golden Fleece

Several sports teams call themselves the Argonauts. The Toronto Argonauts is a football team. At the University of West Florida, both the women's basketball team and the men's baseball team are Argonauts. Why? What does the word mean? We'll discover the answer as we learn about Jason and the Golden Fleece.

• • • • • • • • • • • • •

The story of Jason is at least three thousand years old and has many different **versions.** Here is one of them. Jason was Greek, the son of a king. One day the king disappeared. Jason's mother feared that her husband had been killed. She believed that his own brother, Pelias, was **responsible** for his death. When Pelias announced that he was going to be king, she became afraid he might hurt her small son. She **smuggled** Jason out of the palace. Then she handed the little boy to Chiron, a centaur. Chiron had the body of a horse but the arms, chest, and head of a man. He cared for Jason well and taught the boy everything he knew.

Jason grew up to be a fine young man. He was brave, clever, and strong. When Chiron told Jason that the time had come for him to take away Pelias's job, Jason set off at once for the palace. He **boldly** told his uncle why he had come. Pelias, however, was **cunning** as well as wicked. He pretended to agree to step aside and let Jason be king. But first, he had some advice for his nephew. "The people need to **respect** their king," he said. "So before you take over from me,

bold
cunning
deed
doze
jagged
positive
respect
responsible
smuggle
version

you should do something that will make you famous. You should bring back the Golden Fleece and hang it here in the palace. Then the people will have a king they can be proud of."

Jason knew at once what his uncle was talking about because the Golden Fleece was famous. It was a sheepskin that was made of pure gold. A dragon that never slept guarded it. The Golden Fleece belonged to the king of Colchis, whose kingdom was at the far end of the Black Sea.

Long journeys by sea were full of danger. Pelias knew that Jason would have to sail through a narrow opening into the Black Sea. Then he had to sail past the **jagged** rocks that had sent so many boats to the bottom. He might never reach Colchis. If he did, he might never make it back alive. At least, this is what Pelias was hoping for when his nephew agreed to make the trip.

Jason put together a crew of fifty of the bravest, cleverest, and strongest men in Greece. The name of their boat was the *Argo,* and so the men were called the Argonauts. After many adventures and brave **deeds** by the crew, they reached Colchis. The king of Colchis refused to hand over the Golden Fleece. His daughter Medea, however, fell in love with Jason. She had magical powers and decided to use them to help him. She made the dragon **doze** so that Jason could snatch the fleece away. Together they left Colchis aboard the *Argo.*

After many more adventures, the Argonauts, Jason, and Medea made it back safely to Greece. Because Jason had been gone months, even years, Pelias was **positive** he was dead. Drowned at sea perhaps? Eaten by the dragon? He was very surprised when, one bright sunny day, Jason walked into the palace with the Golden Fleece on one arm and Medea on the other. Jason did become king, and Medea became queen. Sadly, they did not live happily ever after, but that is another story.

Answer each of the following questions with a sentence. If a question does not contain a vocabulary word from the lesson's word list, use one in your answer. Use each word only once.

1. Who was **responsible** for stealing the Golden Fleece?

   _____

   _____

2. What was the greatest danger while sailing into the Black Sea?

   _____

   _____

3. Why was Pelias unable to find the little boy, Jason?

   _____

   _____

4. What did Medea do that was very **bold?**

   _____

   _____

5. Describe one of Jason's brave **deeds.**

   _____

   _____

6. Give an example of Jason's **positive** attitude.

   _____

   _____

7. Why is it likely that Jason's mother did not have **respect** for Pelias?

   _____

   _____

| bold |
| cunning |
| deed |
| doze |
| jagged |
| positive |
| respect |
| responsible |
| smuggle |
| version |

8 How did Medea use her magic power to help Jason?

_____

_____

9 Why might someone else tell the story of Jason differently?

_____

_____

10 How did Pelias show **cunning?**

_____

_____

Fun FACT

• **Bold** people are those who speak or act in ways that make them stand out from others. Do you see how each of the vocabulary words in the passage stands out from the other words around it? That is why **this kind of type** is called _bold_ or _boldface._

responsible

adjective Reliable.

adjective Being the reason for something.

· ·

Word Family

ir**responsible** (adjective)

response (noun)

responsibility (noun)

responsibly (adverb)

Synonyms and Antonyms

Synonyms: dependable, reliable

Antonyms: irresponsible, unreliable

Discussion & Writing Prompt

A chore, such as cleaning your room, is a **responsibility.** What is another **responsibility** you have at home?

2 min.	3 min.
1. Turn and talk to your partner or group.	**2.** Write 1–3 sentences.
Use this space to take notes or draw your ideas.	Be ready to share what you have written.

Study the words. Then do the exercises that follow.

division

n. 1. The act of dividing.

Seth was responsible for the **division** of the pizza into eight equal pieces.

2. One of the parts after something has been divided.

Our team plays in the second **division** of the local soccer league.

3. Something that divides or keeps apart.

This river marks the **division** of the island of Hispaniola into two parts.

 Use a piece of scrap paper to mark the division between you and your partner.

mental

adj. Having to do with the mind.

Mr. Plugovoy asked us to form a **mental** picture of one of our favorite places before we began to write about it.

outcome

n. The way something ends; the final result.

Sylvie read until midnight to learn the **outcome** of the novel.

 Tell your partner the outcome of one of your favorite stories.

pastime

n. Something done to pass the time pleasantly; a hobby or form of recreation.

Aunt Jane's favorite **pastime** is scuba diving.

promote

v. 1. To raise to a higher rank or position.

An important milestone for Dalton was when he was **promoted** to Eagle Scout.

2. To encourage or support; to help bring about.

Talking to the people who live near you **promotes** a friendly neighborhood.

 Discuss with your partner how you could promote exercise in your school.

rate

v. To place in a certain class or at a certain level.

The travel magazine **rated** our state as one of the best places to stay in the summer.

n. A measurement of one thing compared to something else or to what has happened before.

The growth **rate** in our city has increased in the last ten years.

 Talk with your partner about how you rate your top five favorite foods.

regret

v. To feel sorry for something.

My brother **regrets** that he left his bicycle out in the rain because now the seat is soaked.

n. A feeling of sadness or of being sorry.

Dana's one **regret** was that she did not visit her grandparents this summer.

 Tell your partner one thing you regret.

talent

n. A skill for doing something well that comes naturally.

Bella shows a **talent** for imitating other people's voices.

theory

> *n.* An idea or opinion that is used to explain or connect certain facts.
>
> Several facts support the **theory** that a large object hitting Earth wiped out the dinosaurs.

tournament

> *n.* A series of contests in which a number of individuals or teams play against each other to find a winner.
>
> Both my brother and sister play in the town's tennis **tournament.**

15A Words and Their Meanings

Look at the group of words next to the number. Then circle the letter next to the word that has the same meaning.

❶ a form of recreation

(a) regret   (b) rate   (c) pastime   (d) outcome

❷ a feeling of being sorry

(a) talent   (b) regret   (c) theory   (d) rate

❸ a natural skill

(a) outcome   (b) theory   (c) division   (d) talent

❹ something that keeps things apart

(a) division   (b) tournament   (c) rate   (d) outcome

Look at the word next to the number. Then circle the letter next to the group of words that has the same meaning.

❺ rate

(a) to try again   (b) to make up or invent

(c) to feel sorry about   (d) to compare with something

6 theory

    (a) a refusal to give up   (b) an idea to explain something

    (c) a gap in what is known   (d) an excuse for doing nothing

7 promote

    (a) to buy on credit   (b) to follow blindly

    (c) to raise in rank   (d) to lose respect for

8 mental

    (a) related to the mind   (b) related to sports

    (c) related to vision   (d) related to cities

15B   Just the Right Word

Replace each phrase in bold with a single word (or form of the word) from the word list.

1 There were just two players left by the last game of the **series of contests to find a winner.**

2 In the race, my mom came in second in the **group that was set up** for women between thirty and forty years old.

3 We learned the **way the game ended** when we read the final score in the newspaper.

4 After three years with the company, Alan's aunt was **raised in rank** to vice president.

5 How would you **decide which are the likely winners among** the runners in the next race?

6 I **am feeling sorry for** having said those angry words to you.

7 The violinist Midori Goto showed **great skill for playing well** from the time she was a young child.

division
mental
outcome
pastime
promote
rate
regret
talent
theory
tournament

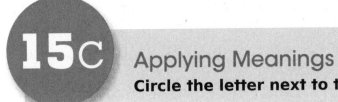

15c Applying Meanings
Circle the letter next to the correct answer.

1 Which of the following is a **theory?**

(a) The Arctic is covered with ice.

(b) Cells are units of living matter.

(c) Elephants weigh more than humans do.

(d) A large object from outer space killed off the dinosaurs.

2 Why do people usually enter a **tournament?**

(a) to sleep

(b) to win

(c) to lose

(d) to rest

3 Which of the following could have an **outcome?**

(a) a diagram

(b) a container

(c) an average

(d) a prank

4 Which of the following is a **mental** activity?

(a) jumping rope

(b) smuggling

(c) daydreaming

(d) gardening

5 When might someone feel **regret?**

(a) after causing an injury

(b) after learning a new language

(c) when enjoying a good book

(d) when doing well on a test

6 Which of the following could be a **pastime?**

(a) finishing homework

(b) doing crossword puzzles

(c) washing the dishes

(d) making your bed

7 What is a common way to **rate** the cities in a state?

(a) by their color

(b) by their taste

(c) by their smell

(d) by their size

Word Study: Antonyms
Look at each group of three words. Decide which two of the words are antonyms and circle them.

You have learned that antonyms are words with opposite or nearly opposite meanings. *Tall* and *short* are antonyms.

1. thrive   promote   discourage

2. timid   gradual   bold

3. cunning   tangled   stupid

4. vacant   smooth   jagged

5. positive   negative   additional

6. frail   careless   responsible

7. hasty   foul   slow

8. scatter   collect   urge

division
mental
outcome
pastime
promote
rate
regret
talent
theory
tournament

Vocabulary in Context
Read the passage.

Sixty-Four Squares and Sixteen Pieces

In most sports, men play against men, and women play against women. Because men on average are bigger and stronger than women, this makes sense. But chess tests the brain; it does not test the body. So why are there national women's chess champions and national men's chess champions? Are men players not as good as women? Are women players not as good as men? Let's try to discover the answer to those questions.

Chess is played on the same board as checkers. The pieces on the board for chess are the king, queen, knight, bishop, castle, and pawn. Unlike checkers, all of the pieces move in different ways. To understand what is happening with each move takes a lot of experience. Luck plays no part in the **outcome** of the game. If you lose, it is because you did not play as well as the person you were playing against.

Some people seem born with a **talent** for playing chess. Often they begin playing at a very young age. Irina Krush, of Brooklyn, New York, is one of them. She was five when her father taught her the rules. By the time she was nine, she was quite good; she could beat her dad easily every time. Chess players know that the best way to improve their game is to play against people who are better than they are. So Irina did this.

She spent an average of five hours a day playing or studying chess, along with going to school. In 1998 she won the title of women's chess champion of the United States. She was fourteen. Her only **regret** was that she did not get to play against men. Three years later she was **rated** among the top one hundred players in the United States. Ninety-eight of them were men.

Chess seems to be mainly a male **pastime.** But it does not start out that way. The number of boys and girls who actively play chess is about equal up to age thirteen. By the time these players go to high school, however, most of the girls have stopped playing. People who try to **promote** interest in chess are puzzled. Why should this be? One **theory** is that to win games in chess you have to be willing to attack as hard as possible. Women, some people say, are better at protecting than they are at attacking. There is a better way to explain the lack of women players, however: There are few role models for girls who want to become serious chess players. This is now starting to change, thanks to people like Irina.

Today more and more schools offer chess lessons. This is where most young players get their start. Once you have learned how to play, you can join a club. Often, there are **divisions** for different levels of players. You will have the chance to take part in **tournaments.** In those contests the result of each game is written down. That gives everyone a record. The more games you win, the higher your name goes on the list. Those at the top are called grandmasters. That is what Irina is now. In 2007, Irina defeated a high-ranking men's player, Vladimir Akopian. And in December 2009, Irina took first in the National Chess Congress tournament. By 2015, she had won the U.S. Women's Chess Championship six more times.

Somewhere today there is a young chess player, boy or girl, who will follow in Irina's footsteps. That person will admire Irina and study her games (a careful record is kept of each one). Then one day that person will come face to face with Irina. Using **mental** power alone, he or she will try to defeat her. That person could be you.

| division |
| mental |
| outcome |
| pastime |
| promote |
| rate |
| regret |
| talent |
| theory |
| tournament |

Answer each of the following questions with a sentence. If a question does not contain a vocabulary word from the lesson's word list, use one in your answer. Use each word only once.

. . . .

1 How are chess players **promoted** from one rank to another?

_____

_____

2 Why are there different **divisions** for those taking part in chess contests?

_____

_____

3 How might Irina feel about so many girls dropping chess at an early age?

_____

_____

4 What else is needed besides **talent** to be a good chess player?

_____

_____

5 Why is playing chess called a purely **mental** exercise?

_____

_____

6 What would be an exciting event for beginning chess players?

_____

_____

7 How does the dropout **rate** for girl chess players compare with that for boys?

_____

_____

8 If Irina played a person new to chess, what would the **outcome** probably be?

_____

_____

9 What are some of the benefits of chess as a **pastime?**

_____

_____

10 Do people know why there are fewer women chess players than men chess players? Explain your answer.

_____

_____

Fun FACT

· ·

- The first **tournaments** were held in France almost a thousand years ago. They were open to groups of knights in armor, who fought each other on horseback in a field. Many people came to watch these contests. The purpose was to give the knights experience in battle.

division
mental
outcome
pastime
promote
rate
regret
talent
theory
tournament

Vocabulary Extension

outcome

noun The way something ends.

Everyone wanted to know the **outcome** *of the race.*

· ·

Context Clues

These sentences give clues to the meaning of **outcome.**

> *Lana was excited to learn the* **outcome** *of her spelling test.*

> *The fans were unhappy about the* **outcome** *of the game because their favorite team had lost.*

> *When you roll a number cube, there are six possible* **outcomes:** *1, 2, 3, 4, 5, or 6.*

Synonyms

result, effect

Discussion & Writing Prompt

If you flip a coin, there are two possible **outcomes**. What are they?

2 min.	3 min.
1. Turn and talk to your partner or group.	**2.** Write 1–3 sentences.
Use this space to take notes or draw your ideas.	Be ready to share what you have written.

Review

Hidden Message Write the word that is missing from each sentence in the boxes next to it. All the words are from Lessons 13, 14, and 15. The shaded boxes will answer this riddle:

At eight o'clock twenty people were in a room. By ten o'clock the room was empty, yet not a single person had left. How can that be?

1. The math problem gave me some good _____ exercise.

2. Our quarrel created a great _____ between us.

3. Maya tried to _____ her kitten into the theater.

4. "The Star-Spangled Banner" is the _____ anthem, or song, of the United States.

5. Are you _____ that you left the keys on the table?

6. The _____ that there was once life on Mars needs to be tested.

7. With no hope of winning, the soldiers will _____ tomorrow.

8. Good eating habits and exercise _____ good health.

9. This _____ proves that we own the land.

10. You can only feel the _____ of downhill skiing by doing it.

11. Her _____ for drawing is clear in this picture she made.

12. Reading was his favorite _____ last summer.

13. The birds will _____ when anyone comes near the feeder.

14. The _____ of growth of our school increased this year.

15. The rabbit used his _____ to escape the fox.

16. She always speaks with _____ to her aunt.

17. I had just started to _____ when the phone rang.